Creating Balance in Children's Lives
A Natural Approach to Learning and Behavior

By

Lorraine O. Moore, Ph.D.
and
Peggy Henrikson

CARREL BOOKS

Copyright © 2005 by Lorraine O. Moore and Peggy Henrikson
First Carrel Books edition 2015

All Rights Reserved. No part of this book may be reproduced in any manner without the express written consent of the publisher, except in the case of brief excerpts in critical reviews or articles. All inquiries should be addressed to Carrel Books, 307 West 36th Street, 11th Floor, New York, NY 10018.

Carrel Books may be purchased in bulk at special discounts for sales promotion, corporate gifts, fund-raising, or educational purposes. Special editions can also be created to specifications. For details, contact the Special Sales Department, Carrel Books, 307 West 36th Street, 11th Floor, New York, NY 10018 or carrelbooks@skyhorsepublishing.com.

Carrel Books® is a registered trademark of Skyhorse Publishing, Inc.®, a Delaware corporation.

Visit our website at www.carrelbooks.com.

10 9 8 7 6 5 4 3 2 1

Library of Congress Cataloging-in-Publication Data is available on file

ISBN: 978-1-63144-008-3
EISBN: 978-1-63144-015-1

Printed in the United States of America

Dedication

The authors lovingly dedicate *Creating Balance in Children's Lives* to Ben, Erin, and Paige and all the children of the world. This book is also dedicated to the teachers, parents, and childcare providers who give so generously of their time and skills to help children grow into happy, healthy adults.

A special thanks to Alice Fowler for allowing us to reproduce portions of the oil painting created by Martin G. Fowler Sr. as cover art.

TABLE OF CONTENTS

Foreword

Chapter 1: Balance for Children in a Changing World __ 1

    What Is Balance? _____ 1
    Changes in Society _____ 2
    Changes in Children _____ 3
    Key Points of Chapter 1 _____ 4

Chapter 2: Progress in Understanding Learning and Behavior _____ 7

    Nature/Nurture Equation_____ 7
    Brain/Heart/Body Interdependence _____ 9
    Emotions, Learning, and Behavior _____ 10
    How the Brain Learns _____ 10
    Nutrition, Learning, and Behavior _____ 12
    New Insights for Children with Learning
      and Attention Difficulties _____ 13
    Key Points of Chapter 2 _____ 15

Chapter 3: Understanding the Dynamic Trio: Brain, Heart, Body _____ 17

    Our Amazing Brain _____ 17
    The Powerful Heart _____ 26
    The Human Body _____ 28
    Key Points of Chapter 3 _____ 29

Chapter 4: The Energy of Emotions _____ 31

    The Internal Processing of Emotions _____ 33
    The Chemicals of Emotions _____ 37
    The Effect of Emotions on Health,
      Behavior, and Learning _____ 39
    Emotions as Intelligence _____ 43

Positive versus Negative Emotions	45
The Importance of Emotional Development	45
Key Points of Chapter 4	46

Chapter 5: Nourishing the Dynamic Trio 49

Basic Needs of the Dynamic Trio	49
Key Points of Chapter 5	66

Chapter 6: The Wheel of Balance: A Model 69

Balance as Wholeness	69
Identifying Children's Needs	73
Balance as the Flow of Energy	74
Considering the Individual	78
Key Points of Chapter 6	79

Chapter 7: Symptoms and Sources of Imbalance 81

Physical Symptoms and Sources	82
Mental Symptoms and Sources Associated with Learning	85
Emotional/Social Symptoms and Sources	87
Guidelines for Rebalancing	89
Key Points of Chapter 7	90

Chapter 8: The Wisdom of Children 93

From "the Mouths of Babes"	93
How Adults Can Help	96
Key Points of Chapter 8	96

Chapter 9:	Options for Preventing and Correcting Imbalances	99
	Needs and Conditions	99
	Options for Enhancing or Creating Balance	101
	Options Presented in Other Chapters	120
	Some Final Thoughts	122
	Key Points of Chapter 9	122

Options at a Glance 125

Glossary 129

Resources 133

- Books 133
- Web Sites 138
- Conferences on Spirituality, Education, and Children 139

FOREWORD

"Balance epitomizes the earth from every perspective, from its elegant celestial minuet to the intricacies of nature's delicate balance. And, certainly if there's one thing that epitomizes humanity's most pressing problems, it's lack of balance."

Jerry Snider, a co-editor of *Magical Blend* magazine (1997, 36)

Throughout the 1990s and into the present, concerns have increased regarding children's learning, behavior, and health. Learning disabilities and diagnoses of attention deficit disorder have increased. Violence in schools is more prevalent. Weight problems and diabetes among children are at an all-time high. General stress levels have risen as a result of fast-paced lifestyles and higher expectations. Many children are clearly out of balance.

Ironically, in the same timeframe, new research has provided breakthroughs about how the brain learns, a better understanding of what triggers specific kinds of behaviors, and greater knowledge about the body relative to health. It is imperative that we now *apply* this new information and understanding for the benefit of children. The purpose of this book is to give educators, parents, and other adults who work or live with children an overview of some of this information, a conceptual model of balance, and ways to bring more balance into children's lives. The results of the scientific research presented here offer both clearer pictures of the problems and possibilities for positive action. Given this research, parents and educators can decide what is most needed in their situations and for their particular children and put appropriate options for balance into play.

Chapter 8 presents the viewpoints of children themselves, offering their own deep insights into how they can help themselves be more peaceful (balanced). These insights also can help adults by showing them the kinds of experiences children need to feel peaceful—which are the kinds of experiences that would benefit us all.

Chapter 9 both summarizes options for balance that are mentioned or implied throughout the book, and it introduces additional options that can be used to help children achieve a balanced state of being. Many of the options are also appropriate for adults, who need to become balanced themselves in order to provide models for children.

Creating Balance in Children's Lives

Each chapter ends with a list of key points presented in that chapter for the purpose of review. Following Chapter 9 is the section Options at a Glance, which lists in short form the options for creating balance that were discussed more fully throughout the text. A glossary of the more technical terms is also provided. For more in-depth information on many of the topics, the Resources section lists additional books as well as Web sites that may be helpful.

The authors commend and thank readers for their interest in helping children to obtain the experiences and resources they need to be healthy, well-balanced individuals who can fulfill their highest potentials.

CHAPTER 1

BALANCE FOR CHILDREN IN A CHANGING WORLD

"You must be the change you want to see in the world."
                                                    Mahatma Gandhi

Children are undoubtedly our most precious asset for the future of the world. The fast pace and unique challenges of modern society have put many children at risk with respect to learning, behavior, and health. Although they are amazingly resilient and pliable, children are also very vulnerable. They are complex beings with specific needs related to their minds, their bodies, their hearts, and their spirits. In order to learn successfully and grow up to be stable, happy individuals, children need the commitment of caring adults to bring balance into their lives. Most often, parents and teachers are entrusted with this privilege. It is the most important job anyone could undertake and a task that helps create a viable future for the human race—no less!

What Is Balance?

Balance is normally associated with words such as equilibrium, stability, steadiness, or harmony. These definitions are true and helpful, but they do not capture the dynamic nature of balance in a complex human being. Maintaining balance among the many functions of a human body and life is an ongoing process that requires awareness and continuous adjustments. It involves achieving internal bodily equilibrium as well as harmony with one's external environment and in one's relationships. Being in a state of balance is always temporary, and rarely, if ever, are all aspects of one's body and life in balance at one time. However, it is possible to attain an overall, general stability that results in physical, mental, emotional, and spiritual well-being.

What would that kind of balance look like? Except for obvious age-related differences, it would look the same in both children and adults. A person in balance is in harmony with himself, others, and his surroundings. He feels good about himself, approaches others with openness and interest, and is creative and productive in his tasks. In this state, his mind has the most ready access to intuition, and he is able to think clearly, solve problems well, and make wise decisions. He has a healthy, strong body with plenty of energy when he needs it for physical activity. When a person is in a state of balance, he is doing what he needs to do with the least amount of effort, while obtaining the highest degree of success. He is able to experience life with joy and tolerance rather than frustration and anger. He can approach challenges and crises with confidence, knowing that the issues can be resolved and he can return to a state of balance.

Achieving a state of balance, and thus harmonious behavior and effective learning abilities, has become more and more difficult given the changes and pressures of today's society. The 21st century heralds unlimited possibilities but also new challenges and problems to solve—all of which can result in stress for both children and adults.

Changes in Society

In her book *Jump Time: Shaping Your Future in a World of Radical Change,* Jean Houston, Ph.D., captures the essence of today's fast-paced society and the envisioned changes for this century. She speaks to both the challenges of "jump time" and the need to confront what she terms "repatterning human nature," or changing the belief systems and ways of taking action that no longer work in a global society. Radical change requires major shifts in human consciousness and demands different skills to navigate and shape the future. For example, Houston writes of the necessity for teaching multisensory skills, values, ethics, and community. She supports a paradigm for education that includes music, drama, and art and embraces experiential learning. She says we must expand our minds and spirits and enlarge our perspectives, and yet with all the expansion, we need to keep returning to our equilibrium. This is the idea of dynamic balance, in which the point of balance, or bar, is continually being raised.

Parents and educators have key roles to play in this repatterning. They are the adults that carry the primary responsibility for modeling and teaching children the skills they need to be successful in this world of rapid change and new possibilities. A balanced lifestyle is now even more crucial.

Chapter 1

Changes in Children

In addition to changes in society, it appears that children are changing. Based on observations, many children are coming into the world with a heightened sense of awareness about themselves and the world around them. Their minds are quick, and often they do well with the new technologies. The basic human needs of today's children are the same as children of a few decades ago, but the means for meeting their needs are now requiring more creative and innovative practices than those generally accepted in today's society.

The means for meeting children's educational needs must also change. According to the most recent information on student learning styles, the ways that children access information and learn about their environments have shifted. Two decades ago, it was estimated that most students were either auditory learners (those that learn best given verbal information) or visual learners (those who learn best through the use of pictures, symbols, etc.). A smaller group of learners preferred a hands-on (kinesthetic) approach to learning. Today, it is estimated that less than 15 percent of students are auditory, approximately 40 percent are visual, and about 45 percent are kinesthetic learners. Thus the vast majority (85 percent) of students in today's schools learn best visually or kinesthetically. These two groups of learners are likely to have difficulty in classrooms where much information is presented verbally. As a result of this shift in learning styles, educators need to consider the degree to which their classroom instruction is verbally-based, and if necessary, adjust to meet the needs of visual and kinesthetic learners.

Besides the change in learning styles, it is now a well-known fact that the mean intelligence quotient of children as a group has risen about five points, as measured by the Wechsler Intelligence Scale for Children, a standardized intelligence test. From this, we can assume that, on the whole, today's children have thinking and reasoning capacities that are greater than those of children 20 years ago. However, at the same time, children's academic skills are declining. Educational psychologist Jane Healy (1999) asked teachers to complete a questionnaire requesting anecdotal information on cognitive changes observed in their students, and she received approximately 300 responses. The following changes were noted by the teachers:

Creating Balance in Children's Lives

- Attention spans among students are noticeably shorter.

- Reading, writing, and oral language skills seem to be declining.

- Students are less able to understand difficult problems in math, science, and other subjects.

These imbalances are being researched and addressed, and some of the new understandings and options are presented in later chapters.

Further exploration is required to determine the educational needs of today's children compared to the needs of children 12 to 15 years ago. Educators must continue to evaluate teaching practices and change them accordingly.

Chapter 2 highlights some of the major breakthroughs that have been made so far in understanding how various aspects of children's lives can contribute to either balance or imbalance. It also presents some of the latest knowledge about how children learn most effectively.

Key Points of Chapter 1

- Maintaining balance among the many functions of a human body and life is an ongoing process that requires awareness and continuous adjustments. It involves achieving internal, bodily equilibrium as well as harmony with one's environment and in one's relationships.

- Balance is even more crucial for healthy, successful functioning in a world of rapid pace and change. Parents and educators carry the primary responsibility for modeling balance and teaching children the skills they need to be successful in today's society of rapid change and new possibilities.

- Children have been changing as well as society. Many appear to have a heightened sense of awareness about themselves and the world around them. Although their basic needs are the same as previous children, meeting their needs requires more creativity and innovation than before.

- Children's most prominent learning styles have shifted from mostly auditory and visual to mostly kinesthetic and visual. For

Chapter 1

the most effective learning to take place, educators must adjust their teaching techniques accordingly.

- Children's mean intelligence quotient has risen, but on the whole, their academic performance has not kept pace. This book addresses some of the possible reasons and remedies for this, but research and observations are ongoing.

Notes

CHAPTER 2

PROGRESS IN UNDERSTANDING LEARNING AND BEHAVIOR

"I find the great thing in this world is not so much where we stand as in what direction we are moving."

Oliver Wendell Holmes

Within the last decade or so, research has brought to light new understandings regarding learning and behavior and what affects children's balance in these areas. This chapter touches on some of these new understandings, which are explored in greater depth in the rest of the book. It takes a look at the latest thinking on the interplay between innate abilities (nature) and environmental conditions (nurture) as well as the interdependence of the brain, heart, and body. It also discusses the key roles that emotions and nutrition play in children's learning and well-being. Finally, this chapter presents some of the latest discoveries in how the brain learns and new insights for working with children who have learning and attention difficulties. An understanding of these areas lays the groundwork for effective strategies for creating balance.

Nature/Nurture Equation

Child development experts have long debated whether nature (innate abilities and characteristics) or nurture (environmental conditions and experiences) has the greater influence on what kind of person a child becomes. Finally, a general consensus was reached that nature and nurture are equally important. Genetics play a large part in the basic structures of the brain and body. The innate plan laid down in the genetic code, or DNA, initially directs the infant's development in stages of increasing mobility, consciousness, imagination, and intellectual understanding of the world and self. On the other hand, outside influences determine what aspects of a child's innate development plan are encouraged or limited. Therefore, development occurs through the interaction of the child with his or her environment and is shaped by the amount and appropriateness of stimulation provided. The foundation laid in infancy continues to be important throughout children's lives and ultimately affects who they become as adults.

Creating Balance in Children's Lives

Given this dynamic interaction between nature and nurture, it is necessary for parents, childcare providers, and educators to be conscious of what experiences best support and enhance children's initial blueprints. We must also recognize that each child's blueprint is unique. This means we need to be aware of not only the normative sequence of development at specific ages, but also where individual children are relative to this sequence in all areas of development.

Future learning and behavior are dependent upon the communication system established during these early years between the cells in the brain, called neurons, and the cells throughout the body. Support for children's development is critical at this time but continues to be significant throughout their school years. The richer the environment during all of these years, the greater the number of interconnections that are made among the neurons of the brain. Consequently, learning can take place faster and with greater meaning if we pay attention to what children need in each step of their development. To be most effective, the timing and amounts of different types of stimuli should coincide with the child's readiness to receive it. This readiness, in turn, depends upon the child's innate blueprint. To push or overstimulate a child creates unwanted stress in his or her nervous system and ends up being not only counterproductive but harmful.

Accepting the nature/nurture balance also means we can no longer consider the child (or nature) to be the only underlying cause for all the behaviors exhibited by that child. We need to give equal consideration to the environment's influence. This viewpoint for living and working with children can be simply expressed as:

$$B = C + E$$

Behavior (physical, mental, emotional, social) = the **C**hild + the **E**nvironment in a dynamic interaction

In practice, this means we need to keep in mind the child's stage of development and provide a balance of stimuli in the areas of physical, mental, emotional, and spiritual development. Excluding one area, such as emotional development, while overemphasizing another area, such as motor development, is not in the best interest of any child. This is especially true for young children.

Chapter 2

Brain/Heart/Body Interdependence

In this age of specialization, the tendency has been to fragment research on human beings into studies of separate functions. Recently, however, researchers have begun to recognize the interdependence of the brain, the heart, and the body, which this book refers to as the Dynamic Trio.

Information emerging from research in the last decade has confirmed the concept of the interdependent nature of thinking, feeling, and taking action. When applied to children, this concept is often referred to as the "whole child" perspective. Examples of study areas contributing to this confirmation include:

- research on the interdependence of mind and body relative to health and the healing of diseases such as cancer

- studies on stress that address the effects of bodily health on emotions, learning, and behavior

- research on the dynamic interaction between the brain and heart and the resulting physiological effects on the body

These and other findings have implications for both children and adults. Neuroscientists and other researchers devoted to studying the physiology of the brain, heart, and body have established the fact that these three components work in concert with each other in complex and interdependent ways. Success or failure in cognitive tasks either contributes to emotional and physical well-being or compromises these functions. What is going on with us emotionally impacts our thinking abilities and body functions. In a similar way, what we do for or to our bodies directly affects our ability to reason and maintain a state of emotional balance.

This dynamic interplay makes it a necessity to view children from the "whole child" perspective. In turn, this perspective will help adults become more aware of ways they can provide conditions and experiences that contribute to a child's balanced state of being, rather than a less productive state of imbalance. Later chapters will explain the brain/heart/body interdependence more fully and give specific recommendations for applying this knowledge to children's lives as well as your own.

Emotions, Learning, and Behavior

The study of emotions, the heart component of the Dynamic Trio, has revealed significant implications for learning and behavior. Until recently, emotions were viewed only from a psychological perspective as consisting of the combination of thoughts and feelings. Then, as scientists became more adept at measuring the effect of emotions on body functions and reasoning abilities, emotions became a topic of extended scientific inquiry. For example, researchers at the Institute of HeartMath®, a nonprofit research and educational corporation in Boulder Creek, California, have validated the powerful effect that emotions have on body functions such as digestion, on heartbeat frequency and variability, and on such thinking functions as mental clarity and decision-making. This results from the fact that the heart and the brain are constantly communicating with each other via the pathways of the nervous system to connect our thoughts, emotions, and body systems. Many emotions start out as physiological responses of the body to external stimuli. They are activated when one or more of our five senses take in information from the environment. The brain's feeling and thinking systems then evaluate the information to determine a response, which can vary from joy or excitement to anger or despair. Once evaluated, the response energetically affects our mind and body either in a positive, neutral, or negative way.

Dr. Robert Sylwester, a leading author and lecturer on the brain and education, states the relationship between emotions and learning this way: "Emotion Drives Attention Drives Learning." Emotions expressed by the mind/body/heart as stress not only compromise learning efficiency but also negatively impact behavior and compromise the immune system of the body. According to researchers who study stress and those who observe trends in health problems, stress has reached epidemic levels among both children and adults in the United States. Chapter 7 will help you determine what factors contribute to increased stress in children, and options to help children achieve a more balanced state of being are suggested throughout this book. Chapter 9 is dedicated solely to presenting strategies for balance.

How the Brain Learns

"How the Brain Learns" was the topic of the November, 1998, issue of *Educational Leadership,* the well-known journal published by the Association for Curriculum and Instruction. The issue was devoted to

Chapter 2

brain research and its implications for children's learning in today's schools. The response to this issue was unprecedented, as demonstrated by the number of requests received for multiple copies. Since that time, many books, articles, and the PBS series "The Secrets of the Brain" have reached the general public.

The task now is to utilize the major findings from this research to improve the learning and behavior of children. The purpose of this book is to help teachers and parents accomplish this task, first by providing an overview of recent information and then by presenting strategies and options that are consistent with the findings of brain/heart/body research. This information also makes it possible to evaluate current parenting and educational practices to see what is compatible, and then to create new practices where necessary to meet the needs of all children.

In the current literature regarding how the brain learns and what types of environments encourage learning, a number of facts occur repeatedly, which can be summarized as follows:

1. The brain learns best when both hemispheres of the brain are engaged in the learning process. (The left hemisphere is more logical and analytical, whereas the right hemisphere is more creative and intuitive.)

2. Learning by making connections between and among ideas and facts (i.e., within a context) is a more effective way for the brain to learn than by processing each fact in isolation.

3. The brain responds well to novelty and input that is varied, such as a multisensory environment.

4. Learning is most effective when the participant is actively engaged as opposed to passively listening and/or watching.

5. The more relevant educational material is to a child's life, the better he/she will remember it.

6. Positive emotions paired with learning experiences provide the brain with meaning and produce greater success in learning.

7. Immediate feedback helps the brain reinforce its neural pathways of information and responses.

Creating Balance in Children's Lives

8. Learning occurs best in a challenging, but safe and nonthreatening, environment that incorporates positive emotional support and a sense of fun and exploration.

9. Learning is most effective when input is provided at a level of difficulty that is appropriate for the child at his or her stage of development.

10. Learning is encouraged when a child is given choices and a degree of control.

11. For optimum stability and effectiveness, a child needs a broad range of skills and interests that are mental, physical, emotional, aesthetic, and social.

12. The brain and the rest of the body need to be supported with a diet that supplies adequate protein, carbohydrates, "good" fats, vitamins, minerals, and calories.

New findings from neuroscience and other scientific research are continually adding to our knowledge to help us understand how the brain learns. In the meantime, parents and teachers are encouraged to build their strategies for working with children on the above assertions. Also refer to Chapter 9 for specific options for rebalancing based on the current data.

Nutrition, Learning, and Behavior

Through scientific research, nutrition has been found to have a direct link to learning and behavior. A balanced diet containing all the necessary nutrients for the brain and body supports learning and appropriate behavior. A diet lacking in nutrients has been linked to poor attention, learning difficulties in the academic subjects, and behaviors associated with hyperactivity, aggression, and depression.

An increase in national concern about our children's health has been triggered by higher obesity rates and a higher incidence of Type II diabetes. Behavioral problems have also been rising, as indicated by the increased numbers of children (down to three years old) that are on some type of medication. A study by a group in San Francisco estimated that as many as one third of our children experience some degree of depression. During the last five years we have also seen a significant increase in violence among our youth. Evidence is now emerging that excessive consumption of fast foods, soft drinks, and sugar products is a contributing factor to these concerns and behaviors.

Since nutrition is now accepted as a science, more researchers are committing their time and resources to studying the relationship between nutrition and learning, and nutrition and behavior. Preliminary findings have shown that nutrition is one of the more promising alternatives to use in treating children with learning and behavioral difficulties in place of or in conjunction with medical treatment. Now parents, caregivers, and schools must be open to learning what they need to know to apply this approach—not only with children who have problems, but with all children to prevent more problems from arising.

New Insights for Children with Learning and Attention Difficulties

In the United States, the National Institutes of Health (NIH) estimates that as much as 15 to 20 percent of the population suffers from one or more of the principal learning disorders. A threefold increase in the prevalence of learning disorders was noted between 1976 and 1993. Attention Deficit and Hyperactivity Disorder (ADHD), for example, has even been called an "epidemic" and the "fastest growing childhood disorder in the United States." Currently, as many as 17.5 million American children cope with learning problems of one kind or another. Knowing both the short-term and long-term challenges these children face in learning and in their personal lives raises concerns for all adults who live and work with children.

What factors are contributing to the significant increase in learning disorders, and what actions are needed to respond to this increasing challenge for children and adults? Fortunately, the scientific, medical, nutritional, educational, and parental communities are addressing these questions and coming forth with some answers. For example, scientists and other researchers at the University of Purdue are involved in the most recent ADHD research. Researchers at Rutgers University are studying learning disability (LD) and related disorders, and the University of Oxford has some of the most recent LD research. Several other universities have also been committing resources to the study of these learning and behavioral disorders.

Neuroscientists have specifically focused on the structure and function of the brain relative to learning and behavioral patterns. Preliminary findings indicate that there are differences in size and metabolic activity in specific areas of the brain when comparing the brain structure and functioning of children with and without some type of learning disability. This research dealt with learning disorders such as dyslexia, ADHD, and autism.

Other researchers, such as Jacqueline Stordy, Ph.D., *(The LCP Solution: The Remarkable Nutritional Treatment for ADHD, Dyslexia & Dyspraxia)*, have focused on the role nutrition plays in these disorders. Stordy addresses the significance of essential fatty acids (EFAs) in children's diets. Insufficient amounts of EFAs contribute to these learning disorders, and supplying the body with EFA supplements can eliminate or decrease the effects of these disorders on learning and behavior.

In his book, *Ritalin Nation: Rapid-Fire Culture and the Transformation of Human Consciousness,* Dr. Richard DeGrandpre puts forth a strong case for the role that culture plays in our nation's disturbing prevalence of inattention and hyperactivity in children. (The book's title refers to the drug Ritalin®, used to treat hyperactivity.) He cites many examples that show how the increase in ADD (Attention Deficit Disorder) among children parallels the hurried lifestyles of today's adults. *Ritalin Nation* challenges us as individuals and as a society to look beyond biological explanations for attention and concentration difficulties such as ADD. Prior to the 1999 publication of DeGrandpre's book, increases in the tempo of life were noted by David Elkind in his book *The Hurried Child: Growing Up Too Fast Too Soon,* in books by J. M. Healy, and in works by other noted authors.

One of the disheartening phenomena accompanying the increase in learning and behavioral problems among children is the widespread use of drugs to treat the symptoms of the problem. A 1996 Drug Enforcement Agency (DEA) report stated that between 1990 and 1996 there was a 500 percent surge in prescriptions for Ritalin. This, along with the published fact that the United States is responsible for 80 to 90 percent of the total Ritalin consumption in the world, is indeed a cause for alarm on the part of all adults who care about what is happening to our nation's children.

Another alarming trend was revealed in a study that appeared in the *Journal of the American Medical Association* (JAMA) in 2000. This study showed a dramatic increase in the prescription of psychotropic drugs to preschoolers. This has happened despite the fact that Ritalin, for example, comes with a warning against its use with children under the age of six. As we consider these trends, we continually need to ask ourselves why this is happening and what alternative treatments for these problems are available.

Some answers are now coming from practitioners who are doing action research and clinical studies in various locales throughout the U.S. in fields such as neuroscience, nutrition, psychology, medicine, and education. Results from these endeavors are supporting the use of nutrition, neurofeedback, movement, sound, color, and relaxation techniques as alternatives to medication for treating children with learning and behavioral problems. It is now up to us to explore these options further and make decisions as to what types of problems and which children can benefit from them. Further discussion and examples of these options will appear in Chapter 9.

Key Points of Chapter 2

- Parents and educators need to be aware of what conditions and experiences children need to support and enhance their genetic blueprints given their ages and levels of development relative to normative patterns. Nature and nurture are equally important in the growth and development of children.

- Research in the last decade has confirmed the interdependent nature of the brain, heart, and body, making it necessary to take a "whole child" perspective in development and learning for a balanced result.

- Stress in both children and adults has reached epidemic levels. Stressful emotions compromise learning, behavior, and the body's immune system.

- Research results are now available on how the brain learns and the types of environments that encourage learning. Educators and parents can base their teaching strategies on these results.

- Fast-paced modern lifestyles can foster inadequate nutrition, which has been linked to poor attention, learning difficulties, hyperactivity, aggression, and depression. Nutritional strategies

Creating Balance in Children's Lives

are helpful in treating children with learning and behavioral difficulties in place of or in conjunction with medical treatment.

- Increases in obesity, Type II diabetes, behavioral problems, depression, and violence in children are cause for immediate concern and action.

- An alarming increase in the prevalence of learning disorders in the United States has been observed. The scientific, medical, and nutritional communities, as well as schools and parents, are addressing factors that contribute to this increase and actions that need to be taken to eliminate or ameliorate them.

- Research supports the use of nutrition, neurofeedback, sound, color, movement, and relaxation techniques as alternatives to medication for treating children with learning and behavioral problems.

CHAPTER 3

UNDERSTANDING THE DYNAMIC TRIO: BRAIN, HEART, BODY

"We are body, mind, and spirit. ... All three aspects need to be present: hands-on, minds-on and hearts-on. ... We do need all three and it is a serious error to think that any of them is 'better' than the others."

Ian Russell, scientist (U.K.)

The more we understand how the brain, heart, and body dynamically interact as energy systems, the more we will see the importance of maintaining a balance among these three components in our daily lives. It is in this state of balance that we are able to access greater degrees of creativity, intuition, and mental clarity—all important components of learning. Within the complexity and beauty of each of these systems and their communication with each other lies the key to bringing more balance into children's lives and also into our own lives. Actions speak louder than words. To be appropriate models for children, we need to be what we desire to teach them.

For our understanding, it helps to have some general knowledge of the functions and organization of the brain, heart, and body, as well as how they work in concert with each other. This chapter provides some basics regarding each component of this "Dynamic Trio," starting with the brain.

Our Amazing Brain

A child comes into the world with about 100 billion brain cells, or neurons, which form the basic structure of the child's brain. Neurons are accompanied by glial cells (neuroglia), which provide supporting tissue. To carry out the brain's functions, the neurons need to communicate with each other, as well as with other cells located throughout the body.

A neuron consists of a compact cell body from which spidery dendrites and one axon extend. Primarily, the neuron receives information from other cells through the dendrites and sends information to other cells through the axon. The junction points where information is transferred between cells are called synapses.

Neurons send and receive information through neural pathways, or networks, by means of electrical and chemical signals. The flow of

Creating Balance in Children's Lives

information within and between these neural pathways is dependent upon the presence and movement of the brain's chemical messengers, called neurotransmitters.

Neural pathways provide the means for cognition, language, visual abilities, motor functions, and emotional/social growth to take place. The initial pathways for these mind/body functions form during the prenatal period. The period from birth up to age five or six is critical for the "wiring" of the brain's neural pathways. The formation of the neural network and connections between cells that allow the flow of information within the brain and to all parts of the body are established through experience and learning. The developing brain needs physical, mental, and emotional stimulation in order to support the neural connections with which a baby is born and to create new connections. These connections are needed for establishing the foundation for future learning and for a child to navigate in everyday life. To accomplish this, it is necessary to provide a variety of experiences that match a child's developmental age throughout the child's growing years. A young child especially needs environmental input, because the young brain prunes weak connections. Insufficient stimulation from the environment during this critical time in the growth of the brain will have a negative impact on a child's future learning performance. The brain in many respects acts like a muscle, in that the more you use it, the stronger and more efficient it becomes.

The plasticity of the brain at any age allows for learning to continue throughout the life span of the individual and makes it possible to change the wiring of the brain. Changes are made through experience and can also be made through technologies such as neurofeedback, specially designed software such as Scientific Learning Corporation's Fast ForWord® program, and auditory stimulation programs created for this purpose. These approaches provide learning and experiences that help form new connections and neural networks within the genetic limitations of the brain's original architecture.

Brainwave States

The brain uses patterns of electrical current to communicate with itself and the rest of the body. These patterns are called brainwave states, or states of consciousness. These states determine our level of awareness at any given time and play a significant role in learning, creativity, inner reflection, and relaxation. For a child to maximize success in a certain task, the child's state of consciousness needs to be appropriate for the demands of the particular task.

Four states of consciousness are associated with brainwave patterns: beta, alpha, theta, and delta. These states exist within a continuum where beta is the waking state, and delta is the deep sleep state. Electrical currents in the brain produce these patterns. They are measured in amplitude (power of the electrical impulse) and frequency (speed of electrical undulations). Frequency is expressed in cycles per second, or hertz, and serves as a measure of electrical activity in the brain at any given time. Each brainwave state contains a range of awareness that affects an individual's state of alertness. This, in turn, affects how strongly and quickly a person reacts physically, mentally, and emotionally to any given situation.

When a person's state of consciousness is on an appropriate level for the stimuli received and the context in which it occurs, a sense of balance is experienced. When brainwave states are mismatched with an activity or situation, a state of imbalance occurs between the sympathetic (arousal) and parasympathetic (relaxation) branches of the autonomic nervous system. This, in turn, causes stress to the mind, body, and heart. In the case of over-arousal, too much energy is expended for a given situation. In the case of under-arousal, insufficient energy is available to meet the demands of the situation. A child in either of these two situations would have a difficult time succeeding.

The chart in Figure 3.1 further clarifies the four brainwave states and their levels of consciousness.

State:	Beta	Alpha	Theta	Delta
Frequency in Hertz:	40-13	12.7	7-4	4-0
Associated Functions:	alertness concentration focus visual acuity	relaxation creativity reflection problem-solving daydreaming	intuition memory fantasy dreaming sleep meditation	deep sleep healing regeneration
Focus:	external world	external/internal world	internal world	internal world

Figure 3.1: Brainwave States and Their Associated Functions

Creating Balance in Children's Lives

All of these brainwave states, or patterns, are important for our everyday functioning and for learning most effectively. Researchers such as Anna Wise have established the concept that the ideal state for learning is that of a "high-performance mind," or an "awakened mind." Wise states that the awakened mind brainwave pattern is a simultaneous expression of all four brainwave states—beta, alpha, theta, and delta. In this state of awareness, the mind is alert and the body is relaxed. It is in this state that the mind can communicate effectively with both the external world and the corresponding internal world of the person. When the body is relaxed and the brain and heart are in synchronization (coherence), the autonomic nervous system is in balance, which helps to free up the higher cortical functions needed for learning. Learning is inhibited when there is either an excess or deficiency of beta in a child's brainwave patterns. When beta waves are excessive, the resulting mental chatter in the brain blocks a child's access to his intuition and creativity and decreases his degree of mental clarity. When beta is low in the profile of the awakened mind pattern, a child has difficulty attending to and concentrating on a learning task such as reading. This brainwave pattern is found in many children who have been given the diagnosis of attention deficit disorder (ADD). For these children, neurofeedback has been used successfully to train the brain to increase beta wave frequency to help increase attention and concentration.

Primary Functions of the Brain

The brain regulates unconscious body functions such as breathing, heart rate, and many forms of movement of which we are unaware, such as the transmission of information. At both the unconscious and conscious levels, the brain receives, organizes, stores, and distributes information to coordinate our actions for present and future use. The brain also regulates our conscious processes of thinking, feeling, and responding to external stimuli.

The 1990s are referred to as the "Decade of the Brain." It is estimated that in the '90s and the previous decade, we learned more about the brain than in all of recorded history. New brain imaging techniques, such as functional magnetic resonance imaging (fMRI) and positron-emission tomography (PET), have provided means for viewing the brain in action. From these techniques, we are gaining new insights about the areas of the brain involved in thinking, feeling, and taking action.

The brain's thinking, feeling, and taking action functions form the basis for all learning and behavior. The areas of the brain that relate to these

Chapter 3

main functions are the neocortex, the limbic (or "mammalian") brain, and the survival (or "reptilian") brain, which includes the brainstem and cerebellum. A functional view of the brain is given in Figure 3.2. It is followed by a discussion of each area in the brain, beginning with the earliest to evolve—the survival, or reptilian, brain—and ending with the neocortex and an explanation of its lobes.

BRAIN FACTS

1 pound at birth • 3 pounds at adulthood • a gelatinous mass with many folds • consumes 20% of the body's energy • a complex information system that uses neural pathways to communicate • transmits information by chemical and electrical means

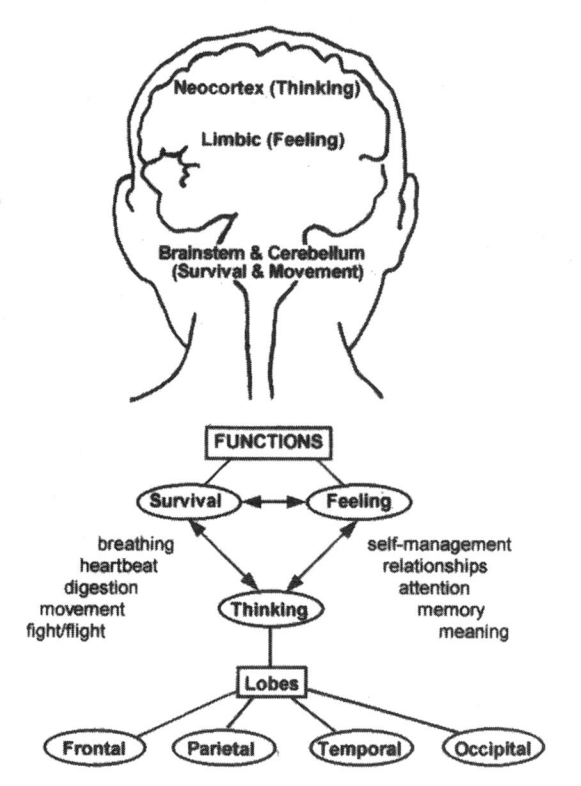

```
           Neocortex (Thinking)
             Limbic (Feeling)
        Brainstem & Cerebellum
         (Survival & Movement)

              FUNCTIONS
         Survival ↔ Feeling
  breathing              self-management
  heartbeat              relationships
  digestion              attention
  movement    Thinking   memory
  fight/flight           meaning

                Lobes
      Frontal  Parietal  Temporal  Occipital
```

F – command center, decision-making, planning, judgment
P – analysis, sensation, language, short-term memory
T – hearing, speech, language, writing
O – processing of visual information

Figure 3.2: A Functional View of the Brain

Acting Functions: The Survival (Reptilian) Brain

Sensory-motor functions are housed in what is referred to as our "reptilian" or "old" brain, the first area of the brain to evolve. This area is around the brain stem and includes the brain stem and the adjoining cerebellum, or "little brain." The primary functions associated with this part of the brain are those functions necessary for the body to survive and protect itself from external threats. The "fight-or-flight" response to danger is activated from this part of the brain.

The function of the cerebellum, a fist-sized structure located in the lower back of the cranium, is now being reappraised. At this point, it is thought to be primarily responsible for balance, motor movement, and some cognitive functions such as the memory of skills that become automatic (e.g., riding a bike).

Feeling Functions: The Limbic (Mammalian) Brain

The second part of the brain to emerge in our evolutionary process was the "mammalian" brain, now most often referred to as the limbic brain or mid-brain. This part of the brain is where our emotions are processed and directed to the neocortex and/or reptilian brain for action. It is also responsible for the production of most of the brain's chemicals. In addition, the limbic system plays a major role in memory and immune system functioning. This part of the brain takes up about 20 percent of the brain's volume.

In recent years, researchers have begun to study more about the limbic system relative to understanding the increased rate of stress and violence among today's youth and adults. Emerging knowledge about the role of emotions in learning, behavior, and health shows promise for helping all children, including children with behavior problems and children with the diagnosis of autism.

Not all neuroscientists agree to the concept of a limbic system that is responsible for emotions. Most, however, agree that certain structures in the brain, namely the amygdala, hypothalamus, hippocampus, and thalamus, are key players in the receiving and processing of emotions. These players are in constant contact with the survival and thinking mechanisms of the brain. In fact, some evidence indicates that the limbic system integrates the three systems (survival, limbic, and neocortex) into a functioning whole. It is thought that the limbic system directs the attention of any one of these systems to the others as needed. It can incorporate the survival function into the service of the thinking function or vice versa. It also can lock thinking functions into the service of the survival system in an emergency, whether it is a real or an imagined one.

For a more detailed discussion of emotions, their processing, and their effects on health, behavior, and learning, see the following chapter.

Thinking Functions: The Neocortex

The part of the brain that emerged last in human evolution is the neocortex, or the cerebrum, which houses our thinking functions. This part of the brain is located at the outer top section of the cranium, comprising 75 to 80 percent of the brain's volume. It consists of the left and right hemispheres, the corpus callosum (connecting fibers between the two hemispheres), and four pairs of lobes. This part of the brain contains the structures that operate at the conscious level of awareness.

The Left and Right Hemispheres of the Brain

In educational settings, certain functions generally associated with the left and right hemispheres of the brain have been commonly used in reference to how children take in, process, and organize information. The left hemisphere is the part of the brain associated with verbal input and language processing. This hemisphere's functions relate to details, the parts and processes of language, and linear patterns often dependent upon specific sequences. Learning to read relies heavily upon these functions of the left hemisphere for the decoding of words, sequencing of sentences, and the correct spelling of words. It is this hemisphere that processes the content of learning. On the other hand, the right hemisphere is associated with the word *gestalt,* which means processing information from whole to part. It represents a global way of viewing and responding to stimuli, i.e., seeing the big picture. The right hemisphere is concerned with visual/spatial stimuli and deals with images, rhythm, and creativity. It provides the context within which the content of learning occurs. Without context, the content aspect of learning consists of isolated facts with no meaning. Applying what we have learned to our daily lives depends upon the comprehension of what we read or hear in the context within which it occurs.

The work of Alan and Nadeen Kaufman (Kaufman Assessment Battery for Children, 1983) measured children's abilities to process information sequentially (left-brain) and simultaneously (right-brain or whole to part). They found that 50 percent of the children used in the normative sample were "integrated learners," combining both left- and right-brain strategies. Of the remaining 50 percent, 25 percent demonstrated a preference for processing information sequentially, and 25 percent demonstrated a preference for processing information simultaneously. This assessment addressed the efficiency with which children took in information and then organized and stored it either sequentially or simultaneously. All children can process information in a number of ways and through all modalities, but a child responds more effectively when new information is presented in his or her preferred processing style. At the same time, the less efficient mode for processing information can be strengthened by providing activities that require the child to use this mode of processing information along with the support of the child's more efficient processing mode. Most of the literature on this topic agrees with the following assertions:

- The brain's left hemisphere is the seat of language, logic, interpretation, and arithmetic. The brain's right hemisphere is the seat of nonverbal processes, visual pattern recognition (faces, lines, shapes), spatial skills, and geometry.

- The left hemisphere governs activity on the right side of the body, and the right hemisphere governs activity on the left side.

The two-hemisphere perspective is useful for helping adults understand how a child perceives, processes, and organizes stimuli. For example, knowing that the right hemisphere usually precedes the development of the left hemisphere, we can design the most effective methods and approaches for working with young children. Based on this knowledge, the most natural way for a child to learn in the early years is through imitation, image, emotion, and movement—all right-brain functions.

Technologies such as the fMRI are useful in discerning the effects that brain trauma and degrees of activity in different parts of the brain have on learning and behavior. Knowing which structure in the brain is not functioning to its fullest capability can help determine strategies to train the child's brain to compensate or, in some cases, correct the functioning of the identified areas.

At this time, most educators and researchers agree that the emphasis should be on whole-brain learning. This means engaging as much of the brain as possible during learning activities and experiences by using music, movement, color, visual aids, and auditory input. This practice is widely being used with children. When the two hemispheres connected by the corpus callosum are in balance and working in harmony, children can most easily fulfill their potential.

The Four Pairs of Lobes

Within the neocortex are four pairs of lobes. Each of these pairs of lobes plays a major role in thinking, or the processing of information, which is central to learning. The approximate location and function of each pair of lobes in the neocortex are shown in Figure 3.3.

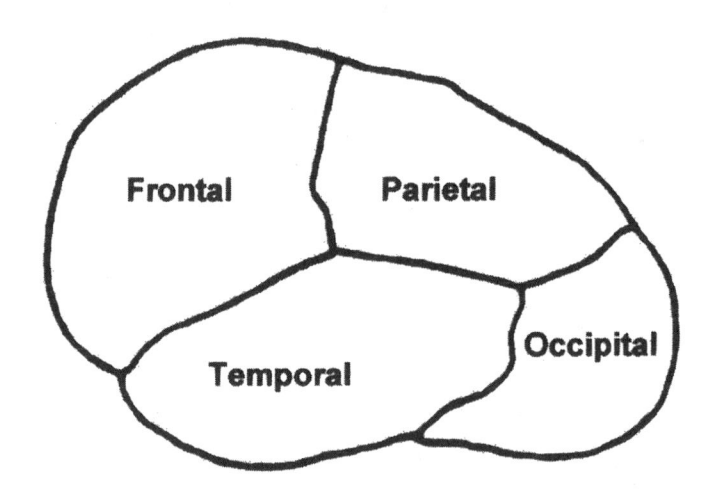

Figure 3.3: Location of the Lobes in the Neocortex of the Brain

The frontal lobes are in an area around the forehead. This area, which includes the prefrontal cortex, is often referred to as the "executive" branch of our brain. The frontal lobes are involved with purposeful acts, such as judgment, creativity, decision-making, and planning.

The parietal lobes are located on the top back part of the head. These lobes have two major functions: to receive information such as touch and temperature from our environment and sensations of pain and pressure from the skin; and to be aware of the location of each of our body parts and its relationship to its surroundings (spatial awareness).

The temporal lobes are located above and around the ears. They are considered the primary auditory areas responsible for the interpretation of sound, pitch, and rhythm. As such, they are linked with hearing, language, and writing. The interpretation of speech is associated with the area of the brain known as Wernicke's Area. This area allows us to comprehend or interpret speech and to put words together in the correct syntax. The translation of thoughts into speech and the development of inner speech take place in Broca's Area (Luria, 1981).

The occipital lobes house the area where visual stimuli are primarily processed. These lobes are located in the lower central back of the brain. This area receives sensory impulses from the eyes and interprets shape, color, and the movement of visual information within space. The visual association areas of these lobes relate past to present visual experience by recognizing and evaluating what is seen (*Smart Moves*, Hannaford).

Other Considerations

Scientists have identified nearly 100 different neurotransmitters in the brain that carry out its communication functions. These transmitters are the chemical messengers of the brain that transmit information between neurons along the many neural pathways of the brain. Neurotransmitters either incite or inhibit the transmission of information to the neighboring neurons. The neurotransmitters often referred to in the literature about the brain include: acetylcholine, epinephrine, serotonin, and dopamine. These will be discussed further in Chapter 4 on emotions.

It is important to remember that all of the brain's structures and functions are interdependent. Each needs the other to exist. When the primary functions of thinking, feeling, and acting are in harmony with each other and in a state of harmony with the body, a person experiences balance. In children, this harmony is reflected in optimal learning and behavior.

The Powerful Heart

The development of the heart precedes that of the brain in a newly formed fetus. For many years, we have known about the biological role of the heart as a pump. As a pump, the heart is responsible for getting blood to all the cells of the body and brain. These cells are dependent upon blood for the oxygen and nutrients they need to grow, develop, and carry out their functions. We now know, however, that the heart is more than a pump, which accounts for only 40 percent of its function.

In 1983, the heart was reclassified as an endocrine gland when it was discovered that the heart secretes specific hormones. These hormones play an important part in the overall functioning of the body.

In addition, biophysicists and other scientists have identified functions of the heart referred to as neural functions. In recent years, neuroscientists have made the exciting discovery that the heart has its own independent nervous system—a complex system referred to as the "brain in the heart." To date, it is estimated that the heart contains at least 40,000 neurons. It is the heart's intrinsic brain and nervous system that make a two-way communication system between the heart and brain possible. Neurocardiology researchers such as Dr. J. Andrew Armour and Dr. Jeffrey Ardell have found that the heart's nervous system is made up of complex ganglia, or nerve fibers. The heart's ganglia contain afferent (receiving), local circuit, and efferent (transmitting) parasympathetic, or relaxing, and sympathetic, or arousing, neurons. Information is carried through this system of nerve pathways to the brain and other processing centers in the body. This communication system is two-way, allowing information from the heart to be directed to the brain and vice versa.

Much has been learned about the heart over the last twenty years, as biophysicists and other scientists have attained more sophisticated technology and measurement devices. In measuring the electrical current generated by the heart, scientists have found it to be 40 to 60 times more powerful than the electrical current emitted by the brain. The heart's electromagnetic field has been found to envelop the entire body and extend out from the body in all directions. This is the most powerful field produced by the body and can be measured by sensitive devices up to 12 feet away from the body. The heart's field of energy interacts with the energy field of the brain as well as the energy fields of other people in proximity.

Research conducted at the Institute of HeartMath clearly supports the emergence of "heart intelligence" as a type of intelligence that plays a significant role in the lives of children and adults. Through the Institute's research and education, we have gained important information about the expanded role the heart plays in our perceptions and emotions. We now have a model for bridging science and public education and for bringing this research into the realm of application. The physiology and dynamics of the heart will be explored further in the chapter on emotions.

The Human Body

The body provides the structures, or gateways, of the eyes, ears, mouth, nose, and skin with which to take in information and respond to the external world. Through its nervous system and spinal cord, the body supports the processing of incoming information and provides the networks necessary for the various brain, heart, and body functions to constantly communicate with each other. Through the body's elaborate circulatory system, all the cells, organs, and tissues are able to receive the nutrients and oxygen they need for survival and growth. Bones and muscles provide for structural stability and movement.

Cells are the basic units of the body. Throughout the body they form an information system that interacts with those of the brain and heart. The Central Nervous System and Peripheral Nervous System are the primary systems for the exchange of signals and information between the brain, heart, and body. We are gaining new knowledge about these complex systems from the scientific community on a regular basis. Practitioners of energy medicine are contributing to this field of knowledge based on experiential evidence. The ancient practices of Chinese medicine have advanced our understanding of the human body as an energy and communication system. As these disciplines add to our knowledge about the human body, it is important that individuals from all the disciplines communicate with each other. Just as there is an information exchange between the brain, heart, and body, there needs to be an information exchange between disciplines to bring theory, research, and experiential knowledge and understanding to the mainstream.

There is more to be said about the Dynamic Trio. Future chapters will further explore the inner workings of the brain, heart, and body as well as the communication that takes place between an individual's internal world and the external world. Looking at children from all points of interaction is key to creating more balance in their lives. Chapter 4 takes a more in-depth look at emotions, and Chapter 5 explores the needs of the brain, heart, and body so we can determine what elements are necessary to support a balanced way of being.

Chapter 3

Key Points of Chapter 3

- The brain, heart, and body continuously interact as dynamic energy systems.

- The period from birth up to age five or six is critical for the "wiring" of the brain's neural pathways. The young brain prunes weak connections. Insufficient stimulation from the environment during this critical time will have a negative impact on a child's future learning performance.

- Four states of consciousness are associated with brainwave patterns: beta, alpha, theta, and delta. These states exist within a continuum where beta is the waking state, and delta is the deep-sleep state.

- All children can process information in a number of ways and through all modalities. A child responds most effectively when new information is presented in his or her preferred processing style (left-brain, right-brain, or both), but the less preferred style can be developed with use.

- The survival (or reptilian) brain handles motor functions and survival reactions; the limbic (or mammalian) brain deals with emotions; and the neocortex houses the thinking functions of the brain.

- Emerging knowledge about the role of emotions in learning, behavior, and health shows promise for helping all children, including those with behavior problems and the diagnosis of autism.

- We now know that the heart is more than a pump. In 1983, it was reclassified as an endocrine gland because it secretes hormones. Neuroscientists have also discovered that the heart has its own independent nervous system—the "brain in the heart." The heart's electromagnetic field is the most powerful field produced by the body. It interacts with the energy field of the brain as well as the energy fields of other people.

- The body provides bone and muscle for stability and movement, and structures for internal and external communications. The body's nervous system provides the means to process information and communicate between the various brain, heart, and body functions. The body's circulatory system delivers nutrients and oxygen to all the cells, organs, and tissues.

CHAPTER 4

THE ENERGY OF EMOTIONS

"Proficiency in emotional management, conflict resolution, communication and interpersonal skills is essential for children to develop inner self-security and become able to effectively deal with the pressures and obstacles that will inevitably arise in their lives. Moreover, increasing evidence is illuminating that emotional balance and cognitive performance are indeed linked."

Research Overview, Institute of HeartMath

Emotions are a dynamic force in our everyday lives. They are always present and changing in response to our internal and external worlds. Recent scientific and social research demonstrates that emotions play an integral role in our learning, behavior, and health. This chapter presents some of the latest research and explains the basic physiology of emotions. It also explains how emotions can either hinder or help the learning process and compromise or support balanced behavior.

Emotions as energy are neutral. It is a person's mental perception of a situation that makes the emotional energy around it become either a positive or negative experience. Thus the brain is intricately involved, as the mind helps determine our emotional reactions. Emotions are shared with others both verbally and nonverbally through facial expressions and body gestures. In a person's extreme response to threat or fear, emotions are observed in the body's posture of fight, flight, or immobilization. The verbal and nonverbal expressions of emotions are the end result of many internal processes interacting in response to internal and/or external stimuli. Children, especially, tend to express their emotions as behaviors, which then need to be interpreted by adults. As we learn more about emotions, we can see that they fully involve all members of the Dynamic Trio—the brain, the heart, and the body.

The word *emotion* is derived from the Latin word *movere,* which means to move. This meaning is evident in the continuous movement of chemicals throughout the body. These chemicals communicate with all the structures of the Dynamic Trio involved in the receiving and processing of emotions and their associated actions. Externally, we see the result of this movement as behaviors we can observe.

Creating Balance in Children's Lives

Today, emotion is given more and more recognition as a key component in the growth and development of children and for the well-being of people of all ages. However, the feeling, or emotional, component of children often is not addressed to the same degree that their cognitive and physical components are. For example, in our educational systems, it is mental development that receives the most attention. At the same time, we are aware of the increase in violence in our nation's schools and communities. This increase in violence has prompted the commitment of more scientific resources to determine the cause(s) for the increase. As violence is directly linked to one's emotional state, emotions have increasingly become the object of scientific study. In fact, this inquiry is now recognized as a biological as well as psychological science. Expanding involvement in the study of emotions has shed new light on them and how they affect children.

The power of love to transform the lives of both children and adults is but one example of the significant roles emotions play in all of our lives. Love, one of our most powerful emotions, has been associated with the heart throughout the ages. The deepest connections we have with each other, the plant and animal kingdoms, and the earth are said to "come from the heart." How often, when we have been in dilemmas, have we heard someone suggest, "listen to your heart" or "follow your heart's lead"? Recent scientific discoveries show that the heart does have an intelligence, and it plays a significant role in helping us to manage our lives and emotions. The Institute of Heartmath has developed tools such as "Freeze-Frame"® and "Cut-Thru"® as well as specifically designed music to help children and adults transmute stress and negative emotions and improve academic performance, behavior, and health. (Refer to the Resources section in the back of the book for more information.)

Through the scientific research conducted at the Institute of HeartMath and other scientific communities, we have gained more knowledge about how emotions affect body functions that impact our health and how emotions direct learning and behavior. The body functions related to blood flow, the digestive system, and the immune system function in concert with each other and with the brain and heart when emotions are in a balanced state. The learning and behavior of children are optimized when emotions are in this state of balance. When emotions are in a state of imbalance, all these functions are compromised.

Chapter 4

The Internal Processing of Emotions

Scientists such as Joseph LeDeaux and Candace Pert and psychologists such as Peter Salovay have made major contributions to our study and understanding of emotions. Psychologist Daniel Goleman brought the role of emotions to the attention of the general public through his book *Emotional Intelligence.* Research has revealed that all the members of the Dynamic Trio play a significant role in the processing of emotions.

Researchers at the Institute of HeartMath study the interacting dynamics of the heart and brain in their approach to the understanding of emotions. As mentioned earlier, the heart has a brain, or nervous system, of its own, and it plays a very influential role in the overall functioning of the Dynamic Trio. Researchers have found that rate of heartbeat variability provides a means by which to measure the autonomic nervous system's degree of balance or imbalance. In turn, the degree of balance between the two branches of this system (sympathetic, parasympathetic) is considered to be an index of the state of balance that exists within the Dynamic Trio. An optimal state of balance exists when the heart and brain are coherent, a state of harmony that exists when the energy systems of the heart and brain are in synchronization with each other.

Neuroscientists have identified the pathways used by the brain, heart, and body for receiving and processing emotional data. Key players in this interaction include the thinking, feeling, and survival mechanisms of the brain, the heart and its connection to the brain via the central nervous system, and the adrenal glands. In actuality, all systems of the Dynamic Trio are involved. However, for our purposes, the following discussion is limited to the autonomic nervous system and the brain structures associated with emotions.

Autonomic Nervous System

To understand the interplay of emotions and their effect on the Dynamic Trio's state of balance, it is necessary to understand the autonomic nervous system (ANS). This system is the part of our central nervous system that is responsible for the physiological functions that operate at an unconscious level (without our awareness). The ANS is considered to be a major system involved in keeping us in balance, a state that exists when the heart and brain are in a state of entrainment, or coherence. As briefly discussed in Chapter 3 on the Dynamic Trio, this system has two main pathways of communication, the sympathetic and the parasympathetic.

The sympathetic branch of this system is the one that is most active when the body is in the fight-or-flight response mode. Adrenaline and noradrenaline are the primary neurotransmitters involved in the action of this branch of the nervous system. When the sympathetic branch of the ANS is highly overactive compared to the parasympathetic branch, the energy of the Dynamic Trio is directed outward for survival purposes. Whether a perceived threat is physical or psychological, an extreme situation leads to compromised thinking ability. This means the brain is not as clear as it could be for mental tasks such as comprehension, decision-making, and problem-solving. Much of the energy needed for such tasks is directed outward to respond to the threat rather than being fully available for thinking.

The parasympathetic branch of the autonomic nervous system is associated with calmness and relaxation. Acetylcholine is the primary neurotransmitter involved in the actions of the parasympathetic nervous system. When the parasympathetic branch of the autonomic nervous system is excessively engaged compared to the sympathetic branch during waking time, a state of passivity and withdrawal occurs, depending upon the degree of imbalance between the two branches. The parasympathetic branch needs to be activated during sleep to promote growth and energy storage.

Stress is a major cause of imbalance between the two branches of the ANS. If stress becomes chronic in a child's life, it negatively impacts his or her health, learning, and behavior. At this point, adult intervention is needed to identify the source/s and seek ways to diminish the stress.

The Structures That Process Emotions

Many neuroscientists have long regarded the limbic system as the brain's principal regulator of emotions. Other neuroscientists prefer to address emotions by studying the structures of the brain and body involved in receiving and processing emotions rather than confining their focus to one system. In either case, there is basic agreement among members of the scientific community that attention and memory are important components of emotions and that specific key structures in the brain are involved in receiving, processing, and responding to emotional stimuli.

The research of the Institute of HeartMath, Candace Pert, and others is now challenging the concept in scientific literature that the limbic system is the "seat of emotions." For example, the Institute of HeartMath takes the position that the heart should be considered a key player in the processing and modulation of emotions. Candace Pert discovered that the heart contains all 200 of a class of neurotransmitters called peptides, which are located throughout the body. She calls the body's peptides "molecules of emotion." Pert maintains that peptides play important roles in modulating emotional states and consequent behaviors. According to Pert, peptides use neural networks, our circulatory system, and air passages to travel throughout the brain and body to modulate a broad range of pleasure and pain. This is a view of emotions that emphasizes a dynamic interaction between the brain, the heart, and the body.

According to Aggleton (1992), research suggests that the amygdala is the principal limbic structure involved in emotional processing. The amygdala consists of two almond-shaped masses located deep within the middle part of the brain. It is the main center for interpreting the emotional content of stimuli received by our senses. It is currently thought that the principal tasks of the amygdala are filtering and interpreting incoming sensory information in the context of our survival and emotional needs, and then helping to initiate appropriate responses. However, when the incoming stimuli are highly charged emotionally, the amygdala can "hijack" (bypass) the reasoning system of the brain, engaging only the survival system of the brain. This puts the fight-or-flight response into full action to deal with the incoming threat from a survival basis only. "This activation of the sympathetic nervous system to a fight-or-flight stress response engages our entire body—the endocrine, immune, circulatory, muscular, and digestive systems." (*A Celebration of Neurons,* Sylwester, 73) Behaviors consequent to this reaction are often aggression (which can be taken to extreme) or withdrawal to the degree of becoming unresponsive to any correction of the situation. For either a child or adult to react to incoming, emotionally charged stimuli in an appropriate, responsible manner, there must be communication between the reasoning brain and the survival brain. If the reasoning brain is bypassed, a feedback loop is formed between the emotional and survival mechanisms of the brain. When this happens to children, an adult must intervene by taking an action that is age appropriate. Because this is a complex task, it is best that adults stay tuned in to children's behavior to recognize when an imbalance may be surfacing and try to ameliorate highly charged emotional situations. Intervening at that point with emotional and/or physical support can ward off an amygdala hijack before it occurs.

The mind and the body do not distinguish between physical and psychological threats in their responses. In children's lives, it is more often a psychological threat, such as insecurity or fear of failure, as opposed to a threat to their physical safety that triggers the fight-or-flight response. Unfortunately, however, physical threats to children have been increasing. Adults should be on the lookout for and try to preempt both physical and psychological threats to children.

The hippocampus adjoins the amygdala in the limbic system. Its credited function is to help our memory processes by relating what is happening now to memories from past experiences. It then converts important short-term memory into long-term or permanent memory.

The hypothalamus and thalamus also assist in regulating our emotional lives and physical safety. The hypothalamus monitors the body's internal regulatory systems and informs the brain about what's happening in the various systems and organs. It maintains a communication link with the prefrontal cortex and a link between the nervous and endocrine systems. It helps in the regulation of the autonomic nervous system as well as the metabolic state of the body. The thalamus is considered a major relay center for incoming sensory information and informs the brain as to what's happening outside of the body. "Most incoming sensory information is sent first to the thalamus, and then it's relayed to the sensory and frontal lobes (in the cortex) for detailed analysis and response. A second, quicker pathway also sends any emotionally laden information from the thalamus to the amygdala (in the limbic system), which uses primitive general categorizations of the limited sensory information it has received to activate an immediate aggressive or defensive response, if the stimulus is sufficiently strong." (*A Celebration of Neurons,* Sylwester, 73)

This information provides a very basic understanding of the structures of the brain that are involved in human emotions. Figure 4.1 provides a summary of these structures and their associated functions.

Chapter 4

Amygdala	Hippocampus	Hypothalamus	Thalamus
primary for emotional processing	evaluates incoming stimuli with regard to existing memories	monitors internal regulatory systems	major relay station for incoming stimuli
filters and interprets incoming sensory info	converts short-term memory to long-term memory	informs brain of activities within the body	informs the brain of external stimuli in action
adjoins hippocampus		links with prefrontal cortex and nervous and endocrine systems	

Figure 4.1: Brain Structures Related to Emotions

The Chemicals of Emotions

Scientists now think that each emotional state involves different chemicals, which trigger different kinds of breathing and body postures. Some serve to calm the body's emotional systems, while others serve to raise the level of arousal in preparation for action. Ratey *(A User's Guide to the Brain)* identifies the four primary emotions of fear, anger, sadness, and joy as universal emotions that exist in all cultures. All other emotions are considered to be a combination of these four emotions.

Figure 4.2 lists seven chemicals in the body and how they are involved in processing and responding to emotional triggers. For example, the neurotransmitter dopamine is a key factor in feeling pleasure, whereas adrenaline is key in a fear reaction.

Chemical	Function/s
dopamine	a neurotransmitter involved with the pleasure and reward centers of the brain/body
serotonin	a mood enhancer, termed the "feel good" neurotransmitter, that appears to effect mood by calming rather than stimulating
endorphins	opiates that prompt good feelings in response to certain behaviors such as relieving hunger, quenching thirst, sex, and running
epinephrine, or adrenalin	acts as both a neurotransmitter and a hormone that puts the body in a state of alert
norepinephrine, or noradrenalin	the primary neurotransmitter for the fight-or-flight response
cortisol (glucocorticoid)	a hormone secreted by the adrenal gland that is a part of the body's stress response—often referred to as the stress hormone
acetylcholine	a neurotransmitter that creates an excitatory connection with cells of the motor cortex (located in the neocortex) for taking action

Figure 4.2: The Chemicals of Emotions

Understanding of the natural chemicals in the human body involved in the processing of emotions is increasing as more scientific effort is being committed to the study of emotions. We will continue to gain knowledge of this complex process as we learn more about the physiological structures and their pathways and how communication takes place in preparing the individual to respond to emotional stimuli. Currently, much of this effort is focusing on adults. There is a need to expand our knowledge and understanding of children's emotional nature so their needs can be met to a greater degree in ways that are age appropriate.

Chapter 4

The Effect of Emotions on Health, Behavior, and Learning

Emotions impact all aspects of our lives—how we feel physically, our behaviors, and our learning. This impact can be positive and support all we do by facilitating our growth and development, or it can be negative and compromise all our functions. We have been underestimating the power of emotions in children's lives and in our own lives. Current research regarding the structures and functions of the Dynamic Trio should be the catalyst to change how we value emotions. This is especially important for children, as emotions play a critical part in their growth and development and how they view the world in which they live. Positive emotional input from caring adults sets the stage and supports a child's physical, mental, and social development, and overall well-being. Negative input or lack of emotional input not only affects the child's physical health but also negatively impacts self-development and relationships with others. It also compromises a child's ability to learn.

Effects and Sources of Stress

Stress is the term used to cover the physiological and psychological effects on the body and mind in response to intense external stimuli such as threats of any kind, too much hurrying, too much pressure to perform, too much excitement, or too much change. The emotions most often caused by a person's mental reaction to stress are those such as fear, anger, and worry. These emotions and their accompanying physiological changes in the body cause imbalances within and between each member of the Dynamic Trio and also cause an imbalance in the distribution of available energy. For example, when most of a child's energy is mobilized externally to cope with a perceived threat, there is less energy available for internal functions, which negatively impacts the immune, circulatory, and digestive systems of the body. The child most often expresses this state of imbalance through aggression or withdrawal. If this state of imbalance becomes chronic in a child's life, the immune system is compromised to the point of creating vulnerability to physical disease. Children in this situation have considerably less energy for play, enjoyment of others, and learning.

A generally accepted fact is that if a child grows up in a loving and supportive environment, that child has a better chance to view self, others, and his/her environment as loving and supportive. Conversely, given the opposite scenario, the child is at risk for viewing self, others, and the environment from a hostile or defensive perspective. In the latter situation, the child is likely to adopt "fight, flight, or freeze" behaviors for survival. Energy is first directed toward survival and secondly toward playing and learning. But no matter what the activity, a child in this kind of situation is often labeled as having "a chip on the shoulder."

There are many potential sources of stress for children. In a national survey on stress among children, Georgia Witkin, Ph.D., from the Mt. Sinai School of Medicine, asked children what stresses them. She surveyed about 800 children between the ages of 9 and 12. The results are published in her book, *KidStress*. The sources of stress that she found among this age group were, according to rank: "school stresses, family worries, peer pressures, the world (pollution, global warming, etc.), the future, and everything." If this survey had been conducted after September 11, 2001, the ranking might have taken on a different order. Also, one needs to reflect on what children younger than 9 and older than 12 might report. Witkin gives us a needed reminder to go to the experts on children's thoughts and feelings—the children themselves. See Chapter 8 for children's thoughts on how they can achieve peace, another word for balance.

To delve deeper into sources of stress in children's lives, we need to take into consideration the impact of current lifestyles and technology, as well as the impact of our global society. The Information Age has given us many conveniences and allowed us unlimited access to information and communication with others, while at the same time contributing to our hurried lifestyle. To support children in all aspects of their lives, we need to temper speed with reflection and relaxation time. This is basic to promoting a balanced way for children to experience their world, and when children experience a balanced lifestyle, they are more likely to achieve a balanced emotional state. As a reminder, we, as adults, need to accomplish this balance first in order to provide the models children need. We need to remember the ancient adage that "actions speak louder than words." Children are very quick to discern when our actions are out of sync with our words. They will act on our nonverbal rather than our verbal behaviors.

Learning and Emotions

Attention and memory are two key components of the learning process. These components can be enhanced or compromised depending upon whether a child's emotional state is one of balance or imbalance. Positive, balanced emotions support a direct pathway to learning in that emotions drive attention, which, in turn, drives learning. Where children

Chapter 4

put their attention, they also direct their energy. When children are excited about an upcoming birthday party or going to a friend's house after school, or when they are upset about something someone said to them, this is where some or all of their attention is directed. Thus the amount of attention and energy available for learning is decreased. A visual image of the direct and indirect pathway to learning appears in Figure 4.3.

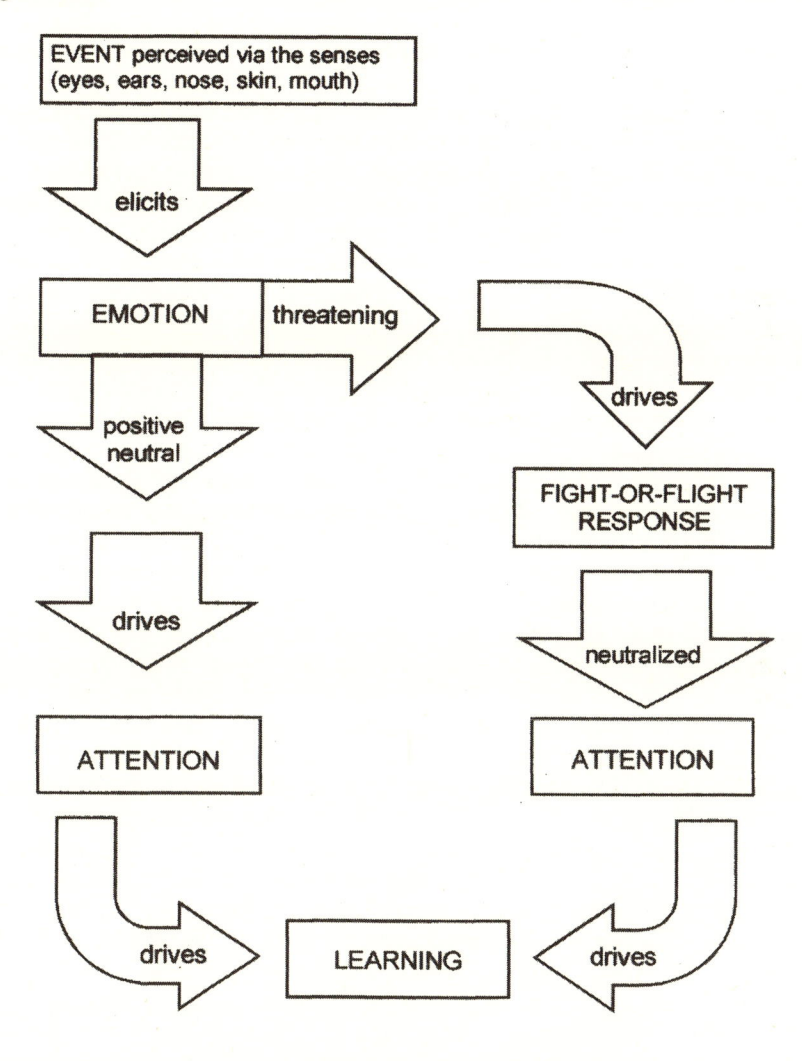

Figure 4.3: Dual Pathways to Learning

Creating Balance in Children's Lives

If a child is not paying attention, he or she is not putting energy into the process of learning, and little or no learning takes place. Being in a balanced state emotionally and free to pay attention to the learning at hand prevents this misfortune. Oftentimes, just taking the time to listen to children and acknowledge what they are excited or upset about can diffuse their emotions to the point where they can redirect their energy to the learning task.

The hippocampus, the structure located in the mid-brain, has the function of converting short-term memory to long-term memory. As noted earlier, this structure is involved in processing and responding to emotions. Under stressful conditions, the body releases a peptide called cortisol. Studies have shown that if an excessive level of cortisol remains in the body for long periods of time, the immune system becomes depressed, the hippocampus's ability to convert short-term memory to long-term memory decreases, and the overall ability of children to learn is compromised.

On the other hand, creating a context for learning that engages the emotions in a positive way increases children's learning by facilitating the transfer of short-term memory to long-term memory. This positive emotional context is important to include in all forms of learning for all ages, but positive emotions paired with learning are especially critical to the learning of young children. The context in which something is learned for the first time is the same context that will be recalled emotionally the next time this learning is encountered by the young child. This is true not only for the learning of life skills but for the learning of preparatory reading, math, and writing skills. The sequential and accumulative learning of any skill always has the potential to take on a positive, neutral, or negative association. For example, if the context and environment in which a child is first taught about numbers is positive, supportive, nonthreatening, and linked to the learner's interest, the next time this child encounters numbers, he or she will have a positive feeling about learning more. And, of course, the reverse also would be true. To quote Carl Jung: "One looks back with appreciation to the brilliant teachers, but with gratitude to those who touched our human feelings. The curriculum is so much necessary raw material, but warmth is the vital element for the growing plant and for the soul of the child."

This section on emotions and learning provides only a brief look at a large and complex field, but it is sufficient to link emotions with learning for the purpose of this book. Many excellent resources on the brain and learning and the part emotions play in learning are available for a more in-depth study of the learning process. Authors such as Erik Jensen, Patricia Wolf, and Robert Sylwester have made this information accessible to the general population.

Emotions as Intelligence

Human beings are not limited to one form of intelligence. They have always had multiple intelligences that have been expressed through music, movement, understanding of self and others, and interactions with nature. However, these abilities were not recognized as intelligences until the 1980s. In American culture, intelligence was largely viewed as involving verbal, quantitative, and visual/spatial abilities. Howard Gardner made a significant contribution to expanding our understanding of human intelligence in his book *Frames of Mind: The Theory of Multiple Intelligences.* Through his work and that of his colleagues who participated in Harvard's Project on Human Potential, we can now take a new look at the meaning of intelligence. Then, we can plan ways to implement the ideas associated with this view to benefit children.

To date, Howard Gardner has identified eight intelligences, two of which are based on emotional and social development. These are referred to as the "personal intelligences," consisting of an intrapersonal intelligence and an interpersonal intelligence. Intrapersonal intelligence refers to one's understanding of self and one's emotions, strengths, limitations, etc., whereas interpersonal intelligence describes one's ability to understand and be in social relationships. Both of these abilities are necessary in children's growth and development and for their learning in a social context, such as in childcare centers, early childhood programs, and school environments.

The idea of an "emotional intelligence" was brought to greater public awareness by Daniel Goleman's books *Emotional Intelligence: Why it can matter more than IQ* and *Working with Emotional Intelligence.* In these books, Goleman expands on the ideas of Peter Salovey, a psychologist at Yale University, who is credited with coining the term "emotional intelligence." Salovey subsumed Gardner's personal intelligences in his basic definition of emotional intelligence and expanded these abilities into five domains. These five domains were further expanded on by Goleman in his first book and brought to the point of application in his second book.

Creating Balance in Children's Lives

The five domains of emotional intelligence include:

1. **Self-awareness**
   Self-awareness is knowing one's emotions or recognizing a feeling as it happens. This is considered the cornerstone of emotional intelligence, upon which most other emotional skills depend. In Goleman's analysis, self-awareness is the most crucial ability, because it allows us to exercise some self-control.

2. **Managing emotions (self-control)**
   This means the appropriate handling of feelings when responding to emotional stimuli, which is necessary for getting along with others.

3. **Motivating oneself**
   Self-motivation is essential for paying attention and is needed for activating and marshaling emotions to work toward a goal.

4. **Empathy**
   Empathy is recognizing emotions in others, a basic "people skill."

5. **Getting along with others (relationship skills)**
   This means managing one's own emotions in the presence of others, understanding others, and knowing the social skills necessary for getting along and achieving social competence in a variety of situations.

Today, there is general agreement among researchers and practitioners who acknowledge the five domains of emotional intelligence as a conceptual framework from which to study emotions and assess emotional and social development. Several questions remain, however, regarding whether these qualities are innate at birth and at what age each of them emerges in the developing child. For example, the fact that often an infant begins to cry upon hearing another infant cry implies that the quality of empathy is present at birth. It is thought that even though all five emotional abilities may be present at birth, both models for the emotional behaviors and contexts in which to practice the associated skills are necessary for the full emergence of each domain. Then the questions arise, if one or more of these abilities do not emerge, can they be taught? At what age? And how? The answers to these questions will surface as more parents, educators, and researchers apply the understanding of emotional intelligence to children of all ages.

Chapter 4

Positive versus Negative Emotions

Since the early 1990s, researchers at the Institute of HeartMath have been studying the physiological, cognitive, and emotional effects of positive emotions such as appreciation and caring in contrast to the effects of the negative emotions of anger and frustration. Among their key findings are: "Different emotions affect autonomic nervous system function and balance in measurably different ways. Anger tends to increase sympathetic activity, while appreciation is associated with a relative increase in parasympathetic activity." (*Science of the Heart,* 17) As noted earlier, the sympathetic and parasympathetic branches of the autonomic nervous system are involved in the physiological processing of emotions, which, in turn, affects the health and learning capabilities of an individual. By measuring heart-rate variability, the researchers found that the physiological effects of anger could be measured in the body up to six hours after the anger had occurred. Given the fact that our behaviors are the result of the interaction of the Dynamic Trio, the consequences of anger can therefore impact a child's or an adult's behavior over a longer span of time than the few minutes during which the anger actually occurred.

The previously mentioned tools developed by the Institute of HeartMath can help children and adults achieve a state of balance where the heart and head are in a state of coherence, which supports an individual's well-being, emotional intelligence, and mental clarity. One of the aspects involved is the use of appreciation. Generally speaking, any technique or method that will help bring children out of negative emotions and into positive ones without judgment will help them achieve equilibrium.

The Importance of Emotional Development

It's a heartening sign that a Surgeon General's Conference on Children's Mental Health was held in Washington, D.C., on September 18 and 19 of 2000. At this conference, mental health was recognized as a critical component of children's learning and general health, and as such, "it must therefore be a national priority." Jane Knitzer, Ed.D., one of the participants at the conference, stated, "Early brain research tells us that the roots of emotional regulation and development, so crucial for life and school success, lie in the earliest relationships. Experience and some research tell us that too many young children are headed for trouble. We must end this disconnect between research and practice." This book is committed to beginning that process.

Creating Balance in Children's Lives

In conclusion, sufficient scientific evidence exists to support the link between emotions, mental and physical well-being, and learning to warrant elevating the importance of the emotional development of children to the level of their cognitive and physical development. All three are needed in a balanced ratio to give children the experiences they require to maximize their learning and development. The ultimate goal for all adults who live and/or work with children is to support them in all possible ways to become who they are meant to be. This involves encouraging the emergence of their strengths, while at the same time helping them to minimize the impact of limitations on their lives.

Key Points of Chapter 4

- Specific key structures in the brain are involved in receiving, processing, and responding to emotional stimuli. However, recent scientific discoveries show that the heart has an intelligence, and it plays a significant role in helping us to manage our lives and emotions. Peptides (chemicals) found in the heart and throughout the body are believed to play important roles in modulating emotional states and consequent behaviors. This view of emotions emphasizes a dynamic interaction between the brain, the heart, and the body.

- We have underestimated the role of emotions, which have powerful effects on the body and on thinking functions. Positive emotional input from caring adults supports a child's physical, mental, and social development, and overall well-being. Negative input or lack of emotional input not only affects the child's physical health but also negatively impacts self-development, enjoyment of life, and relationships with others. It also compromises a child's ability to learn.

- Stress often results in emotions such as fear, anger, and worry. These emotions and their accompanying physiological changes in the body cause imbalances within and between each member of the Dynamic Trio. A survey of 800 children revealed the top two causes of stress to be school issues and family worries.

- Attention and memory are two key components of the learning process. Positive, balanced emotions support a direct pathway to learning, because emotions drive attention, which, in turn, drives learning. Creating a context for learning that engages the emotions in a positive way increases children's learning by facilitating the transfer of short-term memory to long-term memory. This is especially critical to the learning processes of young children.

- The idea of multiple intelligences has brought to wider attention the importance of helping children develop their emotional and social intelligences. Sufficient scientific evidence exists to support the link between emotions, mental and physical well-being, and learning to warrant elevating the importance of children's emotional development to the level of their cognitive and physical development.

Notes

CHAPTER 5

NOURISHING THE DYNAMIC TRIO

"Our mental and emotional diets determine our overall energy levels, health, and well-being to a far greater extent than most people realize. Every thought and feeling, no matter how big or small, impacts our inner energy reserves."

Doc Childre and Howard Martin *(The HeartMath Solution)*

The term Dynamic Trio is used to remind us of the dynamic interaction between the brain, heart, and body. This interaction creates a whole that is more than the sum of its parts, which, in turn, reminds us to think of children as "whole" beings. This chapter discusses what a child's Dynamic Trio needs to be supported and balanced.

Basic Needs of the Dynamic Trio

To maintain the electrical and chemical transmissions responsible for effective internal communications and to support health, learning, and harmonious behavior, the Dynamic Trio needs the following elements on a regular basis:

- **oxygen**
- **water**
- **nutrition**
- **sleep and rest**
- **movement**
- **emotional connections**
- **social relations**
- **sensory stimulation**
- **mental stimulation**

When deprived of one or more of these elements, imbalance occurs and the Dynamic Trio cannot function at its optimum capability. This, in turn, affects how children grow, develop, learn, get along with others, and behave in their various environments. To increase our understanding of this Dynamic Trio, each of these elements will be addressed separately.

Creating Balance in Children's Lives

Oxygen

Without oxygen, the human body can survive for only a few minutes. Breathing in adequate clean air is basic to human survival. Oxygen is required for the body's metabolism to burn food, which is then converted into energy, carbon dioxide, and waste materials. The lungs and heart play a key role in orchestrating this process by transporting oxygen via the blood to all the cells of the body for proper functioning. The quantity and quality of oxygen that children take into their bodies is important for the overall healthy functioning of the body and for supporting the brain's functions. The brain, which weighs about three pounds when fully developed, consumes about 20 percent of the body's oxygen.

Children's concentration, mental clarity, memory, and emotional states improve when the brain receives an adequate supply of oxygen. Encouraging children to develop good breathing habits is a must to help them take in an adequate supply of oxygen. It is important to keep in mind that stress and overexertion result in shallow breathing, whereas relaxation encourages deeper breathing and a more natural pace of breaths per minute. Physical exercise and movement also encourage the intake of more oxygen.

There is increasing concern about the quality of air in the various environments in which children live. This concern relates to the number of toxins in our air, which are bad for the body. Because children have a higher metabolic rate (and thus require more oxygen) relative to body size than adults, they breathe in two to three times as much air. This makes them more vulnerable to environmental toxins, making it mandatory that we pay attention to the quality of the air in all environments in which children live, work, and play.

It is a well-known fact that the prevalence of childhood asthma is on the increase. The symptoms of asthma seem to be triggered by exposure to allergens and air pollutants, including tobacco smoke, home and school dust, molds, and cleaning agents, to mention just a few. This pollution problem is often compounded by poor mechanical ventilation.

A 1995 report from the U.S. General Accounting Office indicated that more than half of our schools have pollution problems. In response to this report, the U.S. Environmental Protection Agency (EPA) and education groups such as the National Education Association have produced the *Indoor Air Quality: Tools for Schools* kit. This kit contains information schools need to detect, prevent, and resolve problems of

Chapter 5

poor quality indoor air. In schools that have acted to correct indoor air pollution, results have been better student learning, higher educator productivity, and less absenteeism of both students and teachers.

Home environments can also be a source for air pollutants. Some of the sources for indoor air pollutants include:

- volatile organic compounds emitted from many home decorating and furnishing products, treated fabrics, plastics, pesticides, cleaners, glues, aerosol sprays, scents, and dry-cleaned clothes

- secondhand cigarette smoke

- gases and soot from inadequately vented gas stoves and fireplaces

- animal dander and dust mites

- mold and other fungi that typically invade the bathroom, basement, and potted plants

- cat litter (NOTE: Physicians recommend that women who are pregnant not clean out cat litter.)

Outdoor air quality is of special concern in heavily industrialized areas, large cities, and other locations with industries that emit pollutants into the surrounding area.

To create cleaner air environments for children, we all need to become aware of the quality of air in the environments where children participate. Many resources are available for learning more about this issue and corrective actions to take when problems are discovered. Check the Resources section of this book for the Web site of the Environmental Protection Agency for a start.

One thing we can all do for children and ourselves is to spend as much time as possible in natural settings—walking, playing, relaxing, and breathing deeply. This gives the body a good quality of oxygen and helps it release the built-up toxins taken in from environments where the quality of air is not as good. This practice will help feed the body's energy system and contribute to a healthier state of balance for children.

Creating Balance in Children's Lives

Water

After oxygen, water is the human body's most important nutrient. Water makes up 70 to 80 percent of the body's composition. It is estimated that water comprises about 90 percent of the brain and about 75 percent of the body's muscles. Insufficient water will cause low energy in the body and may cause muscle cramps. We can live only days if we are deprived of water. This nutrient plays an important role in nearly every major body function, such as regulating temperature, carrying nutrients and oxygen to the cells, removing wastes, cushioning joints, and protecting organs and tissues. Being an electrical system, the body is dependent upon water to provide the electrolyte balance for proper functioning of its cellular membranes.

Adequate hydration is also critical for normal blood flow. It is generally recommended that everyone drink between six and eight glasses of water per day to supply the body's need for water. If the child's activity level is high and/or the climate the child lives in is hot, the child may need a larger quantity of water.

Inadequate hydration is a growing concern for our nation's children. Scientists and nutritionists are studying the link between dehydration and health and learning in children. According to Hannaford *(Smart Moves)*, dehydration is a common problem in school classrooms, leading to lethargy and impaired learning. In schools where children are encouraged to drink more water and carry their own water bottles during the day, improved learning and behavior have been observed. Children of all ages, but especially teenagers, are currently consuming large quantities of caffeinated soft drinks. When pop is the beverage of choice, water consumption decreases. At the same time, since caffeinated beverages act as a diuretic, water content in the body decreases further. It becomes the responsibility of adults who live and work with children to help them develop the habit of drinking water on a regular basis and of using soft drinks as an occasional treat.

Not only is the Dynamic Trio dependent upon sufficient quantities of water but upon good quality water. To nourish the body properly, water needs to be in as pure a state as possible. Chlorine and other chemicals are put into public water supplies to kill bacteria. However, some of these chemicals can be harmful to our bodies, so it is best to drink filtered or bottled water rather than tap water. All children are sensitive to these toxins to varying degrees. Wherever we live, it is good to check the local water supply to determine the quality of the water brought into our homes, schools, and other places of work.

Nutrition

As mentioned in Chapter 2, scientific and nutritional research now supports the fact that good nutrition is essential for health, effective learning, and appropriate behaviors in children. The rise in obesity, Type II diabetes, inattention, hyperactivity, aggression, and depression in children has been associated with consumption of fast foods, soft drinks, sugar products, and unbalanced diets.

The use of medication has become more and more prevalent as a "quick fix." Of special concern is the increased use of medication for behavior problems and depression among children under age five. To what degree the increasing problems can be attributed to the diets of children is still an unanswered question. However, a change in diet has been shown to be a promising alternative to medication in improving children's learning patterns and behaviors. Continuing research in nutrition will expand our knowledge and nutritional strategies in the areas of learning, behavior, and health. The following information lays the groundwork for understanding the role of nutrition in supporting the Dynamic Trio.

The brain, heart, and body are dependent upon certain nutrients to fuel the functioning of their systems. These nutrients are obtained from the major food groups of carbohydrates, proteins, and fats.

Carbohydrates provide the main fuel for the body's energy system. Complex carbohydrates, which are those that release their sugar into the body slowly, are the best type of body fuel. Foods included in this group are vegetables, beans, whole grains, and fruit. These foods, when properly digested, produce a more consistent level of energy than simple carbohydrates, especially when correctly balanced with protein and fats. Simple carbohydrates are starches and sugars that release their energy into the body quickly. This quick release results in spikes of energy followed by a drop in energy, which has a roller coaster effect on the body. Children need to be guided in the amount and the quality of carbohydrates they consume so they can sustain an even flow of energy for their Dynamic Trio to function properly throughout each day. Many processed foods, such as cereals, breads, and boxed or canned foods, contain processed sugar. Reading labels to discern product content has become a must in today's society.

Proteins are often referred to as the body's building blocks. As such, they play a structural and biochemical role in the body, in contrast to carbohydrates, which play an energy role. Proteins provide the framework for every cell of the body. They are needed for the growth and repair of organs, muscles, and other tissues and the production of antibodies, hormones, and enzymes. Proteins also provide the amino acids from which neurotransmitters are made. The amount and type of amino acids in the body affect the efficiency of the transmission of information between neurons and have either an energizing or calming effect on the brain and body. All members of the Dynamic Trio need protein for their structural and biochemical properties. The consumption of some form of protein by children at breakfast has been linked with increased alertness and ability to concentrate at school.

Nutritionists and scientists are showing more interest in studying the amount and kind of fat needed by children in their diets. Based on weight problems and other health concerns, some segments of our society have been moving to low-fat diets. In many situations, this same approach has been applied to children without a scientific basis for doing so. This general shying away from fats in Western diets has not taken into account that there are "good" fats and "bad" fats. Rather than decrease our consumption of all fats, we need to reduce the amount of "bad" fats (processed fats such as margarine and shortening) in children's diets and keep the "good" fats in the form of essential fatty acids and some forms of saturated fats. These have been found to be vital for the structure and effective working of the brain and the nervous, immune, hormonal, and cardiovascular systems, as well as for the health of the skin. Children especially need the correct amount and ratio (about 1:2) of omega-3 and omega-6 essential fatty acids. Children most often get sufficient omega 6 from the foods they eat. Good sources for omega 3 include fish (especially salmon, herring, and mackerel), nuts, seeds, and flaxseed oil.

According to Jacqueline Stordy, "the essential fatty acids are as important to your physical health as vitamins, minerals, trace minerals, electrolytes, protein, and carbohydrates." (79, 80) Based on her research, Stordy further believes that inadequate amounts and an incorrect ratio of omega-3 and omega-6 essential fatty acids can lead to a breakdown in communication between the brain cells of children and lead to the development of learning disorders such as ADHD, dyslexia (a reading disorder), and dyspraxia (a developmental coordination disorder), as well as other neurobiological problems. In addition, low levels of omega 3s in a child's body have been linked to some forms of depression.

In such cases, Stordy and others have been successful in treating these conditions with essential fatty acid supplementation in the form of fish oil, an excellent source of essential fatty acids needed for the brain. Processed fats, such as margarine and shortenings, fall in the category of "bad" fats for the Dynamic Trio. Included here are the fats used in many commercial baked goods. These fats should be used in moderation under all circumstances but especially when children are experiencing learning and behavioral difficulties.

The United States Department of Agriculture (USDA) published the first Food Pyramid in the mid-1980s to serve as a guide for Americans in planning a balanced diet and good eating habits. Research since that time has resulted in new recommendations. Walter C. Willett, M.D., offers a revised food pyramid in the book *Eat, Drink, and Be Healthy: The Harvard Medical School Guide to Healthy Eating,* which Willett co-developed with The Harvard School of Public Health. In this new pyramid, whole grains share the recommended food base with plant oils, to be eaten most plentifully. Red meat, butter, and carbohydrates such as white rice and bread, potatoes, pasta, and sweets share the pinnacle, to be used sparingly. Fruits and vegetables share the second food tier, as in the USDA Food Pyramid, but dairy is given a lesser role and nuts and fish a greater role in the recommended diet.

Using a food pyramid can be a general guide to help plan healthy diets for children and adults. However, the key to this planning rests on the balance of carbohydrates, proteins, and essential fatty acids required to provide the necessary nutrients for the body, which can vary among individual children. Refer to the nutrition books in the Resources section for more information.

Nutrition research has called our attention to the fact that children need some nutrients more than others at certain periods of their lives. For example, it is recommended that fats comprise 50 percent of an infant's diet. The best source is the mother's breast milk, and the next best source is formula that contains the essential fats that infants need. This percentage of ("good") fat, should drop to about 30 percent of a child's intake of calories starting at about age two (USDA, pub. 39). Several studies on childhood nutrition support the conclusion that it is safe to recommend that fat intake be limited to 30 percent of calories and saturated fat intake to less than 10 percent of calories for children of five

Creating Balance in Children's Lives

years and older. The proper amount and kind of fat, along with adequate carbohydrates and proteins, should be a part of every child's diet.

As a general practice, children should be encouraged to eat a variety of food in the amount appropriate for their age and to get plenty of physical exercise. Consideration should also be given to the quality of the food children eat. Natural food that is grown without the use of antibiotics, pesticides, and chemicals provides the best source of nutrients for the healthy growth and development of all children.

When the body receives a variety of quality nutrients, it can function effectively in a state of balance. Imbalance in the body's energy and communication systems occurs when the body receives inadequate amounts or a poor quality of carbohydrates, proteins, and fats. This often occurs when children consume fast foods on a regular basis and/or ingest large amounts of sugar, simple starches, and caffeinated beverages. These foods place a stress on the body, interfering with children's growth and daily functioning. In addition, the calories and saturated fats contained in fast foods contribute to weight problems, which have increased to a point where this issue is now of national concern in the United States. The challenge for us as adults is to address this problem by becoming more aware of what constitutes a healthy diet for children and by modeling healthy eating habits ourselves.

Sleep and Rest

Sleep and rest play a significant role in the body's biological, learning, and emotional processes. Sleep is needed to provide support for growth and development, to restore the body's tissues, and to provide the conditions necessary for consolidating and integrating new learning and memories. Rest in the form of relaxation and a lowering of activity level are needed to bridge the state of alertness and sleep on the wakefulness-sleep continuum.

We are all aware of the effects of a good night's sleep in contrast to a feeling of sleep deprivation. Sleep deprivation compromises our physical, mental, and emotional capabilities and functioning. Until recently, inadequate sleep was overlooked as a factor affecting student performance in school. Chronic sleep deprivation has been associated with severe mood swings, resulting in behavioral and relationship problems, concentration problems, and memory impairment.

Chapter 5

The amount of sleep a person needs is related to age. For example, infants need about 16 hours a day, whereas sleep requirement drops to 10 to 12 hours for children one to three years of age. Then, through the pre-teens, it is normal for children to require 9 to 10 hours. Teenagers generally need 8 to 9 hours of sleep. The quality of sleep is equally as important as the number of hours in achieving sufficient rejuvenation.

Five stages of sleep and their associated functions are commonly known. These stages of sleep recycle themselves several times a night. The sleep stages range from transitional sleep (stage 1) to the deepest sleep (stage 4) and on into stage 5, which is that of Rapid Eye Movement (REM). The time spent in each stage varies by age and individual child. Infants and children need longer periods of REM sleep for the consolidation of rapidly growing neural networks. This stage of sleep is also associated with the consolidation of memories. Recent brain imaging technologies are helping us to better understand the functions of sleep so that we can become more familiar with the signs of sleep deprivation and act to correct them more quickly.

The quality of sleep a child gets is dependent upon the state of balance/imbalance a child is in when she or he goes to bed. Right before bedtime, it is best for the child to avoid lots of activity, scary or fast-paced television shows, caffeinated beverages, and simple carbohydrates. It is also best to make sure a child is not emotionally upset before bedtime. Any over-stimulation interferes with a child's ability to fall asleep, reach the deepest stage of sleep, and stay in the REM stage for a sufficient period of time. In the case of over-stimulation, adults can encourage relaxation of the child's body and mind by playing instrumental music based on 60 beats a minute, reading a relaxing story to the child, massaging the child's feet, or engaging the child in other calming activities prior to bedtime. Be sure to talk through any emotional issues and resolve them. (For music with 60 beats a minute, refer to the book *Superlearning 2000,* listed in the Resources section.)

Rest is a state of reduced activity and relaxation. The body is not meant to function in high gear during the entire period of waking time. It needs periods of low activity, relaxation, and quietness. Over-stimulation of the brain, heart, and body causes stress, resulting in a state of imbalance between the components of the Dynamic Trio. This imbalance then affects the overall functioning of this threesome. In today's fast-paced society, it is imperative to pay attention to the balance between activity, quiet time, and relaxation during waking hours. This balance plays an essential part in the child's ability to pay attention, concentrate, and get

57

along with others. Lower levels of activity can come in many forms, such as looking at books, playing quietly alone with toys, being in a quiet atmosphere with very little stimulation, or just not having to accomplish anything for a period of time. Remember that periodic relaxation and a good night's sleep can do wonders for learning, behavior, and health.

Movement

Many functions of the Dynamic Trio are dependent upon movement. For example, movement is essential for adequate heart and lung development in children, which, in turn, supports brain development. Movement acts as a pump to help the lymphatic system remove toxins from the body. It is also involved in the development of the nervous system, the muscles, and the skeleton.

Many of America's foremost brain researchers met in Chicago in May of 1995 to discuss the link between movement and learning. As a result of this conference and ongoing research, further consideration is being given to the link between movement in early childhood years to readiness skills, the anchoring of learning skills, and overall sensory-motor development. Sensory-motor development forms the basis for learning, motor coordination activities, balance, and the integration of thought into action. As stated by Carla Hannaford, "Movement is an integral part of all mental processing, from the atomic movement that fires the molecular movement that orchestrates the cellular (electrical) movement, to the thought made manifest in action." (*Smart Moves,* 107)

The use of the latest brain imaging technology has clarified the importance of movement for sensory-motor development, learning, growth and development, and health. Ironically, at the same time we have seen an increase in the number of hours infants spend in car seats and a decrease in the physical activity of children of all ages. This appears to be partly due to the fact that today's children spend more time in front of televisions, computers, and video games than did previous generations. As a result, children's health is being compromised, as evidenced by an increase in the obesity rate of children and a similar increase in the onset of Type II diabetes in children. According to Carla Hannaford, Paul Dennison, and others, children's learning is also being compromised by a lack of physical activity. It is time that we, as adults responsible for children's well-being, address this issue.

Chapter 5

Emotional Connections

It is critical that every child's Dynamic Trio be fed with nurturing emotional connections to adults and other children. The Institute of HeartMath refers to "heart intelligence" as an intelligence connected with a person's physiological and behavioral responses to emotions. Studies of children have shown that they need emotional connections for their very survival as well as to grow and develop physically, mentally, and socially. The mother makes the first emotional connection with her child when the baby is in utero. This takes place through the mother's voice, movements, and emotions. As the child enters the world, other adults are also available to provide emotional connections.

Babies and young children who do not have positive emotional connections tend to be less healthy than those who do, and their brains' limbic systems may not develop as they should. The limbic system is an important center for receiving and evaluating stimuli from the external environment and for communicating with the survival brain and the thinking brain. When a child responds to the outside world primarily from a fight-or-flight mode, learning, emotional development, and social skills are compromised. This then places the child in a continuous state of imbalance. Emotional connections need to begin at conception and be continued throughout a child's development. Emotional development in children precedes social development, as development starts from within and moves in an outward, or external, direction.

Social Relations

Children deepen their emotional skills through social situations. They need a variety of experiences with other people to learn how to manage their emotions with others and relate to people within a broad spectrum of activities. Social contacts are also a way of bringing meaning into children's lives. Interaction provides a way for children to understand themselves and develop healthy relationships. Social contacts help the limbic system balance the reasoning and feeling parts of the brain. Just as much time needs to be devoted to children's emotional and social abilities as to their physiological and cognitive development.

Sensory Stimulation

Everything comes into our awareness energetically. Our five senses of hearing, sight, taste, smell, and touch help us take in, process, and respond to environmental stimuli. Each sense responds to a different

Creating Balance in Children's Lives

form of energy, such as sound waves, light waves that take on color and shape, ingredients in food, all varieties of aromas, degrees of warmth, and types of texture. Each form of energy has its own frequency and intensity of vibration. It's important that children have the opportunity to experience all these forms of energy through their senses.

Sensory stimulation helps lay down the neural pathways for the body's various communication systems and promotes the growth and development of all the body's functions. Relative to this development, Carla Hannaford reminds us that the integration of sensory systems is just as necessary to consider as incoming sensory information. According to Hannaford, it "is the integration of sensory input which gives us information about gravity and motion, and about our body's muscular movements and position in space. These play a surprisingly significant role in our awareness of the world and also in our ability to understand and learn." (*Smart Moves,* 33) Thus learning is dependent upon each of our senses as well as how these senses interact to complete the many complex tasks in which children engage. To develop these senses, children need experiences that stimulate each of the senses and also experiences that require the integration of senses, such as seeing and hearing or sensing gravity and motion while at the same time connecting with the body's position in the space around it.

Movement plays a critical role in this integration of all the senses. Exploring one's environment and engaging in play are two natural ways in which children get sensory-motor experiences. Children who have difficulty or who are unable to perform activities and skills that come easily for other children are often referred to a physical therapist or an occupational therapist trained in sensory-motor therapy for a sensory-motor evaluation. If it is found that a child has a sensory-motor impairment, a variety of strategies are available to lessen or correct the area/s of dysfunction.

Rudolph Steiner and others have expanded our view of the senses to include not only outer senses but inner senses, such as self-movement, balance, and language. Another of our inner senses is intuition, which is receiving increased attention. The holistic perspective that considers both inner and outer senses provides a comprehensive way of viewing children. This chapter discusses the five outer senses of hearing, vision, touch, taste, and smell. Careful nurturing of these senses will greatly enhance a child's development and capacity for learning.

Chapter 5

Hearing

Children are born into a world filled with sound. A variety of sounds, from soft music to jets taking off, are present 24 hours a day. Unlike our eyes, our ears cannot be closed to stop input. They remain open and working even while we sleep. Our ears act as the main ways for the body to receive sound for aural processing, but growing evidence exists that the entire body is sensitive to sound. This is based on the idea that all cells in the body have vibratory properties and thus are capable of being sound receptors. Sound impulses in the form of heartbeats resonate throughout our bodies.

External and internal sounds (heartbeats) are produced when something vibrates, either randomly or in a periodically repeated motion. These sounds are graded according to decibel level (degree of loudness). The higher the decibel level, the louder the sound. One decibel (1dBA) is one degree of loudness on a continuum of sound, where zero represents the average least perceptible sound. Examples of decibel ranges in everyday life, from quiet to loud, are illustrated in Figure 5.2.

LOWEST									HIGHEST
								Jet engine takeoff	
							Live rock music amplified		
						Loud thunder			
					Busy traffic				
				Vacuum cleaner					
			Chirping birds						
	Moderate rainfall								
	50	60	70 - 75	75 - 85	120	90 - 130	120 -140		

Decibel Level

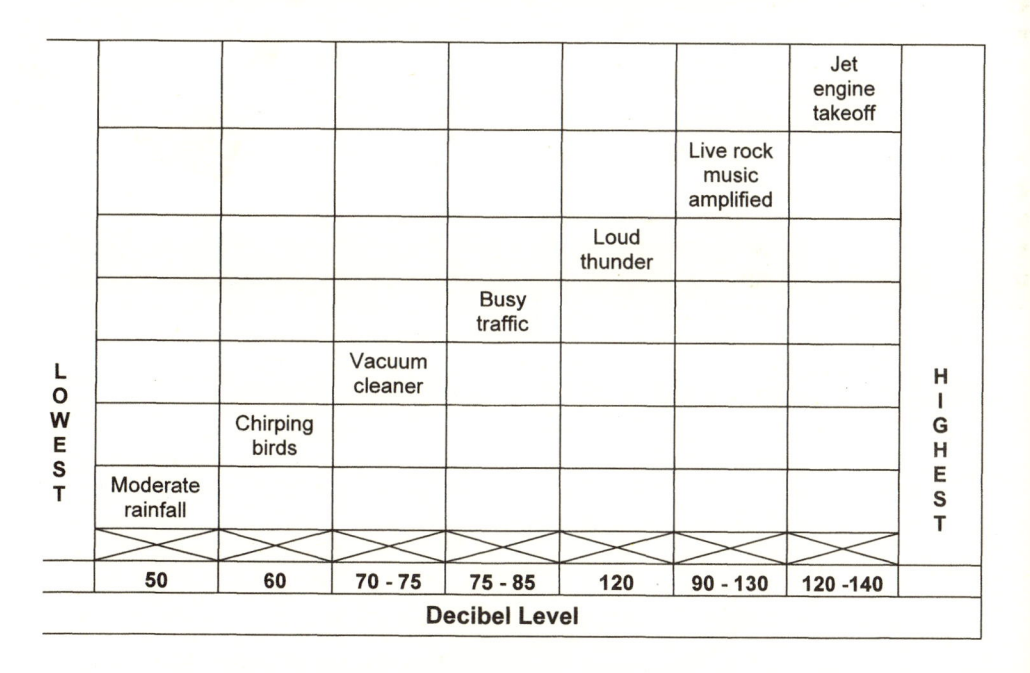

Figure 5.2: Examples of Sounds and Their Decibel Levels

Creating Balance in Children's Lives

Concern has increased among health practitioners, educators, and parents about the effect of too much and excessively loud sound on children's hearing, health, and learning. Listening to music with settings on high bass and high volume (especially with earphones), the booming qualities of digital sound, and the increase in environmental noise are thought to be contributing to an increase in hearing difficulties.

For example, studies have been conducted to measure the effect of airplane noise on children's health and learning. Children living close to airports were found to have higher blood pressure than normal and compromised academic achievement. More studies of this kind need to be conducted, as well as studies on the effect of noise pollution in large cities and other high-density industrial areas.

On the other hand, healthy sounds within an appropriate range are needed for the growth and development of children's aural processing and listening skills. Healthy sounds also contribute to bringing the Dynamic Trio into greater degrees of balance, harmony, and relaxation. We need to monitor as best we can the sound environments of children and teach children to become aware of what sounds are healthy and what sounds are not.

Vision

In utero and during the first few months of infancy, the development of vision proceeds at a slower rate than that of hearing. When children are born, they need appropriate visual stimulation to promote the growth of the neural pathways and patterns in the brain necessary for seeing and interpreting visual images. According to recent studies in sensory access to external stimuli, the majority of environmental stimuli are accessed through the eyes. It is well recognized that we are a visually oriented society.

To achieve effective vision, children need to develop peripheral and focused vision simultaneously. They also need to develop flexibility in shifting their eye movements from near to far and side to side. Excessive TV watching and playing of video games can narrow a person's range of vision at any age. This narrowing decreases visual adaptability to the environment and in learning situations. A state of chronic stress can also limit a person's visual field by making it less adaptable to the task at hand (Dennison).

Children should be exposed to a variety of visual stimuli, such as various shapes, images, patterns, and colors. Encouraging children to play with or manipulate various objects helps integrate their visual and tactile senses and gives them a deeper understanding of what they are seeing. Spending time in nature is one of the best ways to receive balanced visual (and auditory) stimulation.

Creating inner images, or mental pictures, is another skill that needs to be nurtured. Inner vision is not as dependent on concrete objects and experiences as outer vision. The use of inner vision enhances the imagination of children by having them create in their minds what something might or could look like without the distraction of external stimuli. Reading stories without pictures and having children picture what the words are saying is one way to develop imagery in children.

A balanced approach to stimulating vision includes not only the correct amount and type of visual stimulation but also a balance in the child's activities so that the Dynamic Trio's needs are met.

Touch

Studies have shown that positive human touch is critical for children's initial survival in the world and continues to be important for their physical growth and development. According to Mary Carlson, a neurobiologist at Harvard Medical School, hugs are as vital to the health and development of infants as food and water. Touch in the form of massage, hugging, holding, and playing with children helps to balance stress hormone levels and increases growth hormones, promotes maturity of the nervous system, stimulates all the senses, and promotes social development. Human touch is a vital way to make emotional connections with other people. As noted earlier, the emotional development of children is dependent upon forming these connections.

Besides lots of hugs, one way to help satisfy the Dynamic Trio's need for human touch is with hand and foot massages. The hands and feet are points where many of the nerves of the human body converge. Massaging children's hands and feet provides a soothing form of physical contact as well as an emotional connection with someone who cares. Back rubs are also soothing and may help restless children fall asleep at night.

Creating Balance in Children's Lives

Taste

Taste allows children access to a more satisfying connection with the nourishment needed for physical growth and development. It also can provide a source of pleasure by linking a positive emotional experience with food.

According to the ancient Ayurvedic tradition of holistic medicine in India, including six categories of taste in one's diet will develop the full range of taste and meet the body's needs. The six categories are: sour, bitter, sweet, salty, pungent, and astringent. Most foods fall into the sweet category, but the others are needed for balance. In the Ayurvedic tradition, foods are used to maintain balance or to heal imbalances in the body, although one needs to study this science to see which foods do what. Examples of foods in each of these categories include:

- **sour**—yogurt, cheese, green grapes, raspberries, lemons, limes, pickles

- **bitter**—rhubarb, dandelion root, turmeric, coriander, fennugreek, goldenseal

- **sweet**—wheat, rice, milk, sugar, beef, fish (general), oils (general), melons, corn, oats

- **salty**—sea salt (and table salt, but sea salt contains additional beneficial minerals)

- **pungent**—onion, radish, chili, garlic, black pepper, mustard, ginger, cinnamon

- **astringent**—pomegranate, celery, lettuce, spinach, legumes, sage

Many foods fulfill the need in more than one taste category. For example, chicken, butter, eggs, kidney beans, apples, bananas, and peanuts are sweet and astringent; sesame oil and carrots are sweet, bitter, and astringent; and oranges are sweet and sour.

With taste, as in other areas, the idea is to give children a wide range of experiences so the result is an overall balance.

Smell

Scientists tell us that our sense of smell, referred to as the olfactory sense, was the first to develop in the evolution of our species for the purpose of survival. Our sense of smell is unique in that it has a direct pathway to the brain. It does not need to pass through what is referred to as the blood/brain barrier. This makes the use of aromatherapy effective in treating the emotional states associated with depression, agitation, and anxiety. The calming effects on the body of certain aromas can be helpful for children with hyperactivity. In fact, aromatherapy can help the Dynamic Trio reestablish an overall state of balance, or homeostasis.

The sense of smell has a strong emotional component, in that every fragrance and odor is attached to a feeling state, resulting in either a positive, neutral, or negative reaction. Positive or neutral reactions either reinforce or maintain the Dynamic Trio's state of balance. Negative reactions can trigger imbalance, as they may call up stressful experiences for a child.

Mental Stimulation

The 100 billion neurons that each child has coming into the world become activated through stimulation. Learning and responding to the world are dependent upon the number and patterns of neural networks available, so children must be given opportunities to develop these networks. The more enriched the environment, the more networks are developed. Remembering that nature and nurture have an equal impact on a child's development, it is our responsibility as adults to provide children with the necessary nurturance.

The Dynamic Trio needs to be given a daily diet of a variety of activities and experiences that stimulate the capacities of its interacting systems. Just as it is important to feed the mind, heart, and body with oxygen, water, nutrition, rest, movement, emotional and social connections, and sensory stimulation, it is important to provide the Dynamic Trio with daily mental stimulation. Children need many and varied activities to exercise their thinking and reasoning abilities in order to continually create new neural pathways for learning and to strengthen existing pathways. For very young children, these activities can take the form of exploring various objects in the environment by engaging the five senses in concrete ways. As children progress developmentally, the stimuli need to be designed to accommodate each child's readiness and capacity for involvement. To accomplish this, it is a good idea to maintain a balance between the concrete and the abstract, to combine active and reflective participation, and to build in a success factor by giving the child activities that you know he/she can do as well as those you know will be a challenge for new learning.

We now have considerably more information about how the brain, heart, and body work together than we did even five years ago. We also know more about what this Dynamic Trio needs to grow and develop to its full capabilities. Now is the time to take action and make changes based on this increased awareness. The first action we need to take is to evaluate our current practices to determine if they reflect the latest knowledge about how children grow, develop, and learn. If a practice no longer fits with the data, it needs to be discarded, clearing the way for practices that reflect what children need to maximize their state of "wholeness." The next step is to explore the options for practices that reflect the new data, verify these options for practicality and scientific support, and then implement the practices that are possible and practical given individual situations. Change is necessary, and children deserve our best efforts. Chapter 9 offers a wide range of verified options to help make this process easier.

Key Points of Chapter 5

- Oxygen is required for the body's metabolism to burn food for energy. In addition, children's concentration, memory, mental clarity, and emotional states improve when the brain receives an adequate supply of oxygen.

- Air pollution is a concern in both homes and schools, and children are more vulnerable to airborne toxins than adults. A 1995 study found that more than half our schools have indoor air pollution. In schools that have cleaned up their air, results have been better student learning, higher educator productivity, and less absenteeism of both students and teachers.

- After oxygen, water is the body's most important nutrient. Water makes up 70 percent to 80 percent of the human body's composition and plays an important role in nearly every major body function. Dehydration is a common problem in school classrooms, leading to lethargy and impaired learning.

- The Dynamic Trio needs carbohydrates, protein, and fats. Carbohydrates supply energy, protein plays structural and biochemical roles, and "good" fats are vital for the structure and effective working of the brain and the nervous, immune, hormonal, and cardiovascular systems, as well as for the health of the skin.

- Sleep is needed to provide support for growth and development, to restore the body's tissues, and to provide the conditions necessary for consolidating and integrating new learning and memories. Chronic sleep deprivation has been associated with severe mood swings, resulting in behavioral and relationship problems, concentration problems, and memory impairment.

- Children need a balance between activity, quiet time, and relaxation during waking hours. This balance plays an essential part in their ability to pay attention, concentrate, and get along with others.

- Movement is crucial for adequate heart and lung development, which, in turn, supports brain development. Movement helps the lymphatic system remove toxins from the body and helps develop the nervous system, muscles, and skeleton.

- Children need emotional connections for their very survival as well as to grow and develop physically, mentally, and socially. Emotional connections need to begin at conception and should be continued throughout a child's development.

- Children deepen their emotional skills through social situations. Social contacts help the limbic system balance the reasoning and feeling parts of the brain. They are also a way of bringing meaning into children's lives.

- Sensory stimulation helps lay down the neural pathways for the body's various communication systems and promotes the growth and development of all the body's functions. A variety of sensory stimulation should be provided for children, but care should be taken to avoid extremes, such as loud noises, on any regular basis.

- Learning and responding to the world are dependent upon the number and patterns of neural networks available. The more enriched the environment is in terms of mental stimulation, the more networks a child can develop.

CHAPTER 6

THE WHEEL OF BALANCE: A MODEL

"Optimal health is defined as a balance of physical, emotional, social, spiritual, and intellectual health."

American Journal of Health Promotion (1989, 3)

The state of balanced being and doing is the birthright of all children and adults. Although it is not easy to achieve, it is much more likely if one is aware of what inhibits balance and what contributes to it. It helps to have a working model. This chapter presents a model for balance that can be used as a conceptual framework for the many aspects involved in achieving this state of being and doing. The model acts as a bridge between our current knowledge and its application. It can be changed or expanded upon as experience and research add to our understanding of the meaning of balance, especially as it applies to children.

Balance as Wholeness

Balance is dependent upon harmonious interaction within and between a person's mental, physical, and emotional/social functions. Elizabeth Kubler-Ross, M.D., adds a fourth dimension—that of spirituality. She refers to these four human functions as the "four quadrants" that make up a whole individual. To achieve a state of inner balance and to realize one's full capabilities, all four quadrants need to be nurtured and expressed. In Figure 6.1, this wholeness concept of balance is portrayed visually as a wheel.

Creating Balance in Children's Lives

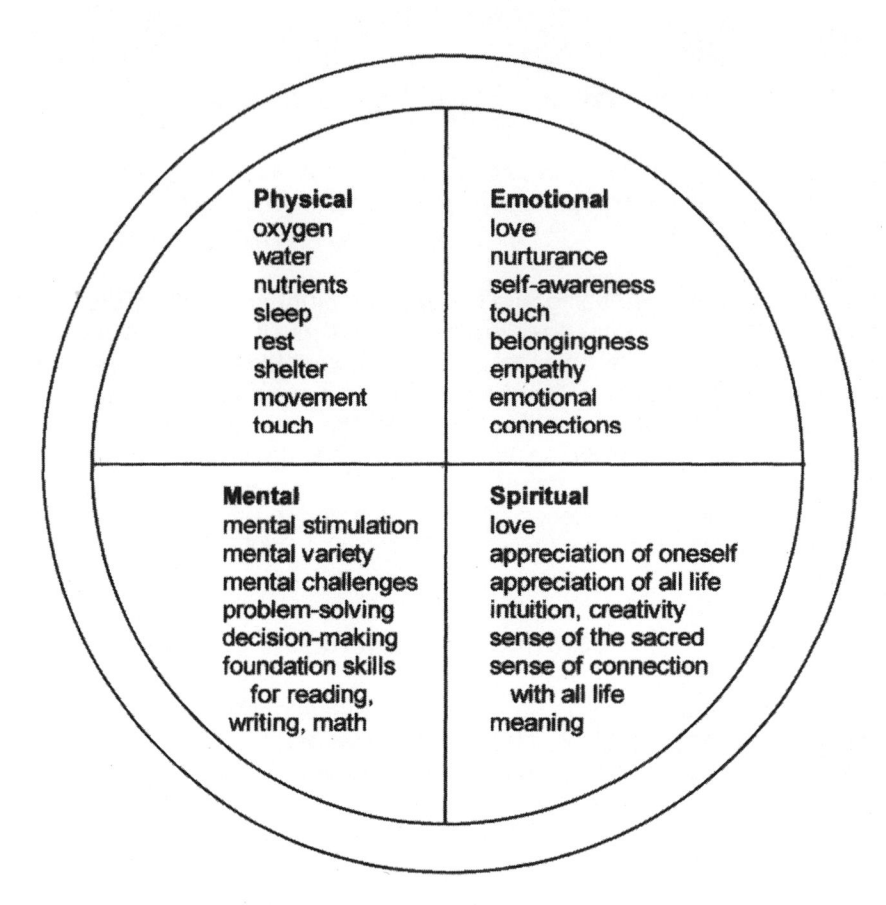

Physical oxygen water nutrients sleep rest shelter movement touch	**Emotional** love nurturance self-awareness touch belongingness empathy emotional connections

Mental
mental stimulation
mental variety
mental challenges
problem-solving
decision-making
foundation skills
  for reading,
writing, math
	Spiritual
	love
	appreciation of oneself
	appreciation of all life
	intuition, creativity
	sense of the sacred
	sense of connection
	  with all life
	meaning

Figure 6.1: Wheel of Balance Model

When this wheel has sufficient energy in each quadrant, it can roll freely with a minimum of effort, making it possible to roll uphill and over rough surfaces as well as on level, smooth, and downhill surfaces. Let's apply this concept to children. When children are in a balanced state of being, a state of wholeness, it becomes possible for them to move in their external environments with the greatest degree of readiness and satisfaction. However, if any of the components of the quadrant are undernourished and/or not expressed, a state of imbalance occurs. The wheel under these conditions takes on an irregular shape and becomes wobbly. Following are some examples of this state.

Chapter 6

When an overemphasis is placed on a child's physical and mental, or cognitive, development at the expense of his or her emotional and spiritual development, the child's ability to function and maneuver is compromised. The child's wheel would look like Figure 6.2.

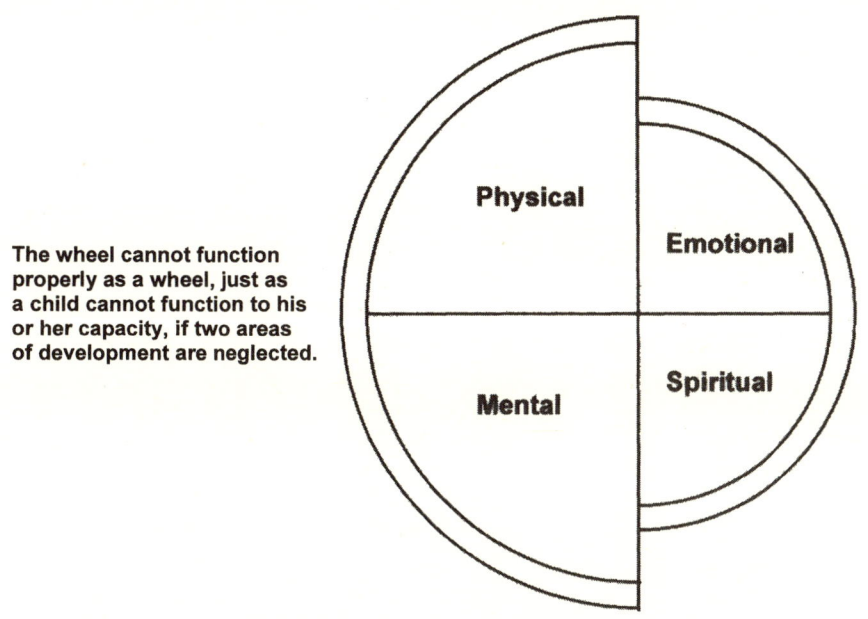

The wheel cannot function properly as a wheel, just as a child cannot function to his or her capacity, if two areas of development are neglected.

Figure 6.2: Overemphasis on Physical and Mental Development

Children are dependent upon adults to have their needs met in a holistic way. Unfortunately, in today's society, children's emotional needs are not met to the same degree that their cognitive needs are met. The spiritual dimension of children is not addressed to any significant degree in most educational environments. "Spiritual" in this context is not to be equated with religion but rather with the yearning of children for meaning in their lives and the expression of this meaning through thoughts, feelings, and actions. In order to allow the child to experience his or her life and the world in a meaningful way, the inner spirit of each child requires acknowledgment and nourishment. Even though the spiritual dimension is not acknowledged in public schools, it is addressed in educational venues such as Waldorf and other private schools. In addition, attention is beginning to be paid to this dimension of children through books on this topic and a major conference that was held on education and spirituality in the fall of 2003 and 2004. (See Conferences on Spirituality, Education, and Children in the Resources section.)

Creating Balance in Children's Lives

Overemphasizing the cognitive development of children at the expense of the other three areas results in a wheel shape that is depicted in Figure 6.3.

Little movement is possible from this wheel. Children experiencing this configuration would tend to act from a highly intellectual perspective, limiting their physical, emotional/social, and spiritual development.

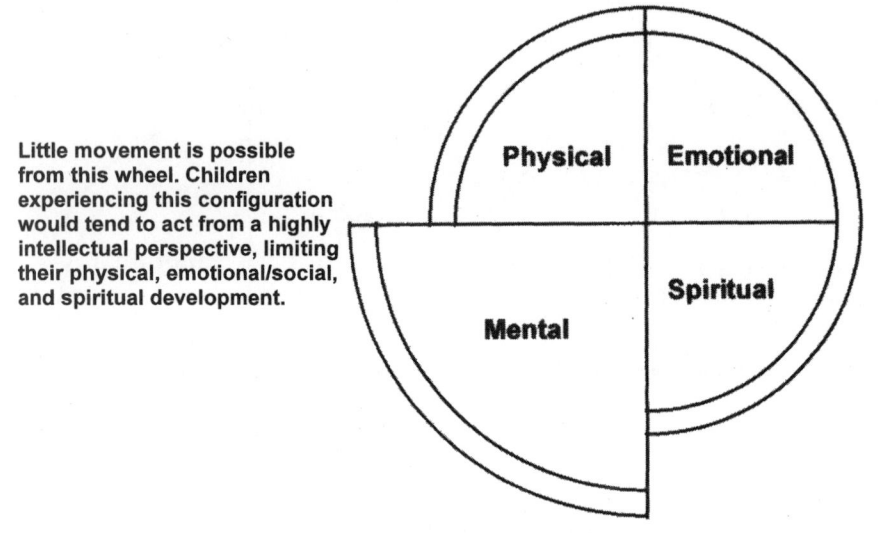

Figure 6.3: Overemphasis on Mental Development

If children perceive and act from a highly developed cognitive ability without the interaction of the other areas, over time they become alienated from their own inner selves, from others, and from society at large. For such children, everything would exist in an abstract realm rather than a realm representing the richness of all facets of life.

Developing the foundation for this inner balance begins with the growing fetus. The mother must be as balanced as possible herself, as her state intimately affects the state of the fetus. This requires awareness on the part of the mother, who must address each of the four quadrants in a holistic way. The foundation for inner balance continues to be built as the child grows, so all adults who live and work with children need to develop this awareness. Our practices for parenting and educating children should reflect this understanding of the "whole child." In education, this means that schools should focus on the needs of children in planning appropriate curricula, in their teaching methodologies, and in how progress is measured rather than focusing only on the academic curricula to be taught and test results. This focus will ensure that children's physical, cognitive, emotional, and social developments mature in a balanced way. Using the wheel metaphor, this means a much smoother ride through life for children rather than a wobbly or unstable one.

Identifying Children's Needs

To accomplish this balance for all children, we need to have an understanding of how they grow and develop and progress through the various stages of maturation. It means we need to be aware of what children require from us as adults along the continuum of development, recognizing that children arrive at and complete each stage according to their own individual timeline. We know that children in general share similar characteristics and have some of the same needs at various ages, while at the same time each child has unique characteristics and needs. The blueprint for the unfoldment of each child is carried in the individual's DNA, or genetic code. It is then up to the adults in children's lives to provide the necessary experiences and environmental conditions to shape and encourage the emergence of children's skills and abilities. The younger the child, the more responsibility adults have for supporting this shaping. As children grow, they gain in their ability to use their inner resources to nurture their own development.

Many books are available that address the developmental stages of children's growth. The last section of this chapter enumerates some of the individualistic aspects of children that need to be considered. Their shared needs are discussed below.

Basic Needs

The metaphor of the wheel and its four quadrants is offered as a working model to be further developed and used as a basis for living and working with children of all ages. To put this model into practice, it is necessary to become familiar with its many facets and dimensions. The needs listed within each quadrant of the Wheel of Balance (Fig.6.1) are basic for all children. They are not meant to be prioritized by the order in which they are listed. However, in working with these needs, it may be helpful to be familiar with the basic needs that psychologist Abraham Maslow included in his Theory of Motivation as a reference point. Even though these needs are often listed in a hierarchical order within the form of a pyramid, Maslow did not intend that one had to be met before the next one emerged as a motivating force for behavior. In the dynamics of working with children, it is natural that we respond to many of the needs

Creating Balance in Children's Lives

listed simultaneously. The needs that Maslow considered basic for all human beings are listed in Figure 6.4.

Aesthetic Needs	need for beauty
The Desire to Know and Understand	curiosity and learning
Self-Actualization Needs	psychological growth and the development and utilization of potential
Esteem Needs	self-respect and esteem from other people
Belongingness and Love Needs	love, affection, and belonging
Safety Needs	physical and psychological safety
Physiological Needs	air, water, food, sleep, and shelter

Figure 6.4: Maslow's Basic Human Needs as a Basis for Motivation

Inherent in the Wheel of Balance Model are the environmental and social conditions of the society in which a child lives. These conditions vary among different cultures and different parts of the world, as well as within the United States. They need to be taken into account when considering the degree to which each of the needs are to be met in order for children to grow and develop. Needs in this situation should not be equated with what we consider to be a certain standard of living.

As we become aware of what children need to live more balanced lives in this fast-paced society, we must initiate and implement ongoing ways for supplying these needs. To do this, we must recognize the fact that balance is both a state of being at a particular time in a particular situation and an ongoing, overall process.

Balance as the Flow of Energy

There are many facets involved in the dynamics of balance. First, viewing the human body as an energy system is basic to understanding the dynamics of balance, its complexities, and the many aspects involved in developing a working model of balance.

Chapter 6

As a human energy system, the mind, body, and heart are constantly receiving and sending out energy. One of the keys to maintaining the Dynamic Trio and bringing about a balanced state of being is maintaining an advantageous ratio of incoming to outgoing energy. If a person gives out more energy than is taken in over an extended period of time, the person's energy system becomes depleted, causing a state of imbalance. This compromises the ability to engage in daily tasks to a sufficient degree and may mean not being able to participate at all in some tasks. It also is important to maintain a reserve of energy for times of crisis and when high expenditures of energy are needed.

Children are especially vulnerable to depletion of the energy they need to grow physically and perform their daily tasks. Sources of energy for children come from meeting their basic and growth needs in all four of the quadrants. Adults who live and work with children must become aware of what types of nutrients, environmental conditions, emotional connections, and experiences bring energy to children and what depletes their energy. More on this topic is presented in later chapters.

The Principle of Yin/Yang

In addition to the ratio of incoming to outgoing energy, there is also the matter of bringing the interplay of "opposites" into harmony with one another. In Western society we tend to think in terms of dualities or opposites rather than bringing two extremes on a continuum into harmony with one another. For example, we use the words *sad* and *happy* to describe our feelings, when in actuality we are somewhere on the continuum between the two. These two feelings are part of the same emotional system, and one could not exist without the other.

The principle of yin/yang can be useful in understanding the interplay of opposites that govern the workings of all forms of life on Earth as well as human affairs. The energy involved in this interplay extends both inward and outward to every level of life, from the subatomic to the cosmic. If we understand the principle of yin/yang and how to apply it to our daily lives, we can become more aware of what is needed to adjust circumstances for the best interests of children's growth.

The energy of yin represents concepts such as completion and contraction, and the energy of yang represents concepts such as creation and expansion. Included are any other pair of polarities that are complementary opposites and could not exist without the other. When these polarities are integrated with their complement, a state of balance

75

Creating Balance in Children's Lives

is achieved. This state of balance can best be described as the "middle way." The principle of yin and yang is used in macrobiotic cooking for preparing and balancing foods in one's diet, in feng shui for balancing energy in one's environment, and in movement arts such as yoga, tai chi, and qigong for balancing one's internal system of energy.

Besides achieving balance, the idea is also to maintain a flow of energy, which requires being aware of where energy is blocked or polarized so that it can be released. We need to recognize, however, that certain circumstances require more energy from one polarity and less energy from the other. During these times, a shift from the middle way toward one of the two poles takes place to accommodate what is necessary to adapt to a specific situation, task, or person. Upon completion, the shift in energy should be back toward the middle—a state of equilibrium—ready for the next action.

In applying the yin/yang principle of balance to children, we should consider the various needs of children, the functions they perform on a daily basis, and the qualities required for their development. Examples of these appear as continuums in Figure 6.5. Please note that not all of these examples are opposites per se, but they are aspects of children's lives that need to be balanced in relation to each other.

Chapter 6

Middle Way

thinking	<<<	>>>	feeling
talking	<<<	>>>	listening
doing	<<<	>>>	being
giving	<<<	>>>	receiving
waking	<<<	>>>	sleeping
aggressive	<<<	>>>	passive
structured	<<<	>>>	unstructured
limits	<<<	>>>	no limits
linear/sequential	<<<	>>>	creative/intuitive
stimulated	<<<	>>>	relaxed
known	<<<	>>>	unknown
work	<<<	>>>	play
loud	<<<	>>>	soft
visual	<<<	>>>	auditory
alone	<<<	>>>	with others
predictable	<<<	>>>	unpredictable

Figure 6.5: Continuums of Balance

To accomplish the task of guiding and supporting balance in children, adults must use their intuition as to what a particular child might need and be willing to try something different if a certain approach doesn't work. Most importantly, they must be willing to look at their own states of balance and imbalance and make corrections when necessary. This is a prerequisite in order to raise our consciousness to a level where we can be appropriate models for children.

Energy Flow Between Brainwave States

One of the considerations in working with any model of balance is the degree and type of energy that a task or interaction requires. For example, both reading for information and playing competitive sports require a focused concentration on external stimuli that is characteristic of the beta brainwave state. (See Figure 3.1.) However, the amount of physical energy required for competitive sports is far greater than it is for reading for information. If one were to remain in this state of heightened awareness during a time when relaxation or sleep was required, the over-arousal of the Dynamic Trio would make it difficult or impossible to relax or go to sleep. In contrast, if one were in an alpha state of awareness and faced with the demands of learning or competitive sports, one would not have the mental or physical focus for the task at hand.

The effectiveness of the state of awareness or arousal relative to a given task or situation can be readily observed in our children's classrooms. Children who are more successful in their learning and in their relations with others generally have a closer match of their arousal level to the situation than those who are less successful. Part of the trick of being in balance is to be able to shift from one end of a continuum to the other when necessary and back to the middle again to maintain an overall balance. Adults can help children make this shift by using the various options discussed in Chapter 9 and by modeling appropriate behaviors.

The Heart as Leader in Balancing Energy Flow

According to the current research about the strength of the heart's energy, the heart takes the lead in producing balance among the members of the Dynamic Trio. This research and resultant theory is a direct challenge to the previously accepted theory that the brain does the leading. To assist in the application of this research, neuroscientists and educators at the Institute of HeartMath have developed the tools mentioned in the previous chapter that children and adults can use to bring their focus of attention to the heart. The key to improving balance in the mind, heart, and body is to engage the mind in positive feelings by focusing on the heart.

Considering the Individual

In considering balance as wholeness and balance as a flow of energy, we have been addressing the characteristics and needs of children overall, but each child also has unique characteristics and needs. In living and working with children, attention must be given to meeting both their shared and unique needs. To identify the unique qualities and needs of a child, it helps to keenly observe and really listen to the child as an individual.

Factors to take into consideration are each child's:

- age
- gender
- culture and context
- special talents
- developmental or behavioral challenges
- temperament
- personality

Child development specialists have studied children of all ages for a number of years. These studies have provided us with documentation of behaviors generally associated with various age groups, which gives us a foundation for understanding, being, and working with children. This knowledge is critical for the setting of expectations and being aware of behaviors that signal a balanced state of being or an imbalanced state of being. When behaviors signal an imbalance, our responsibility is to work towards correcting the imbalance for a particular child within the possibilities of his or her unique genetic blueprint. Then, each child has the opportunity to grow and develop toward his or her potential. To assist in this endeavor, the following chapter discusses symptoms and behaviors that are indicative of imbalance.

Key Points of Chapter 6

- Balance is dependent upon harmonious interaction within and between a person's mental, physical, emotional/social, and spiritual aspects. A model of balance can be portrayed as a wheel. When all four of these aspects, or quadrants of the wheel, are nurtured and expressed, the wheel can roll smoothly. If any aspect is over- or underemphasized, the wheel will be wobbly, and the child will not have a smooth ride through life.

- Adults need to have an understanding of how children normally grow and develop and progress through the various stages of maturation, so they can determine if and when imbalances arise.

- The mind, body, and heart are constantly receiving and sending out energy. One of the keys to maintaining the Dynamic Trio and bringing about a balanced state of being is maintaining an advantageous ratio of incoming to outgoing energy.

Creating Balance in Children's Lives

- Adults must become aware of which nutrients, environmental conditions, emotional connections, and experiences bring energy to children and which deplete their energy. Fulfilling any of the needs mentioned in this chapter will enhance their energy.

- The ancient principle of yin/yang can best be described as the "middle way" in the interplay between opposites. The idea is to achieve an overall balance of activity or experience on the continuum between any two opposites or extremes. It is also to maintain a flow of energy, which requires being aware of where energy is blocked or polarized.

- Research shows the heart takes the lead in producing balance among the members of the Dynamic Trio, in direct challenge to the previously accepted theory that the brain does the leading. The key to improving balance in the mind, heart, and body is to engage the brain in positive feelings by focusing on the heart.

- Attention must be given to meeting both the shared and unique needs of children in order to promote balance. Consider each child's age, culture and context, special talents, developmental or behavioral challenges, temperament, and personality.

CHAPTER 7

SYMPTOMS AND SOURCES OF IMBALANCE

"Today's child has become the unwilling, unintended victim of overwhelming stress—the stress borne of rapid, bewildering social change and constantly rising expectations."

David Elkind *(The Hurried Child)*

It is a challenge for children and adults alike to maintain a state of balance during these unbalanced times. Much insecurity exists in our lives, as we continually face the threat of terrorism, violence in our schools, economic uncertainty, expectations to achieve, an accelerated pace of living, and the unlimited stimulation that constantly bombards us from various media. Perhaps more than any other time in history, children need our love and nurturing, along with ways to help them stay balanced so that relationships, learning, behavior, and overall well-being are not compromised.

All forms of imbalance, whether they are physical, mental, or emotional, result in stress on the body. Because the body, heart, and mind are so interconnected, all the Dynamic Trio's systems and functions are negatively affected. This, in turn, jeopardizes children's learning and behavior. Children who are in a chronic state of stress have difficulty learning and behaving in appropriate ways, and they tend to get sick more often. It is best, of course, if adults can become aware of the sources of the stress and work to prevent or ameliorate them before the symptoms appear. Sometimes, however, certain behaviors or symptoms of stress appear first, and we then need to work backwards to figure out the sources.

Behaviors and symptoms associated with imbalance and stress are many and varied. They can manifest physically, mentally, and/or emotionally. The forms they take depend upon the ages, temperaments, and environmental circumstances of the individual children involved. This chapter presents an overview of the physical, mental, and emotional indicators of imbalance in children in terms of behaviors and symptoms that might be observed. It also provides a process for discovering the sources of imbalance.

Creating Balance in Children's Lives

Physical Symptoms and Sources

Our bodies are energy systems, and they need fuel in the form of nutrients and oxygen to carry out their daily functions. When the body is in balance, enough energy is available to perform tasks, engage in age-appropriate activities, and still have some energy in reserve. When a child has insufficient energy to get through the day, it indicates an imbalance of some kind within the body, mind, or heart. Since the low energy is first observed at the physical level, it is appropriate to begin looking for the source of imbalance at the physical level. Other physical symptoms of stress/imbalance include: excessive energy, frequent colds and other illnesses, a general state of lethargy, problems breathing, irritability, eating problems, sleeping problems, frequent headaches, and frequent stomachaches.

The following series of steps can be taken to sort through potential physical sources of stress, identify the problem, and determine ways to alleviate the problem.

Step 1: Identify the behavior or symptom that is indicative of an imbalance in the body, such as frequent headaches.

Step 2: Look for and identify any potential physical sources of the problem by asking a series of questions to help pinpoint what needs to be changed in the child's lifestyle, diet, or environment. Some basic questions to consider include:

- Is there a healthy mix between activity and relaxation? Too much of one and not enough of the other can result in too great an expenditure of energy or a lack of energy.

- What is the child's diet like? Fast foods, processed foods, too many sugary or caffeinated soft drinks, or an improper ratio of proteins to fats to carbohydrates given activity levels can cause an imbalance in the body.

- Does the child get enough quality sleep to rejuvenate the body? Insufficient or poor quality sleep results in chronic tiredness and irritability and puts stress on the body.

- Does the child drink enough water, get sufficient exercise, and have an opportunity to breathe in good quality air

Chapter 7

every day? An insufficient amount or poor quality of any of these can trigger an imbalance in the body.

- Does this child have a negative reaction to certain chemicals and other toxins in his or her environment? Chemicals and even seemingly innocuous substances or ingredients in food can trigger allergic reactions, deplete a child's energy, cause breathing problems, or any number of physical symptoms—all of which put the body in a state of stress.

- Are there any other, perhaps unusual, situations that the child physically encounters or experiences?

Step 3: Document the frequency of the symptom or behavior that you, another adult, and/or the child are concerned about by creating a chart. Record the frequency of the symptom or behavior as well as the circumstances in which it occurs. This should be done before making any changes in the child's diet, lifestyle, or environment to establish a baseline of frequency with which to compare, once changes are made. An example of this type of chart appears below in Figure 7.1.

Targeted Symptom or Behavior: _____

Day / Date Monday ___/___/___	Time 00:00 (a.m. or p.m.)	Circumstance
Etc.		

Figure 7.1: Initial Frequency of Targeted Symptom or Behavior

Step 4: Create a plan of action to change the behavior or symptom that you want to rebalance. (See Chapter 9 for options.) If you have observed more than one behavior/symptom you want to change, choose the one about which you are most

83

concerned. Once you begin to decrease that problem, the other problem/s may also decrease in frequency. Your plan will be based on what you and/or another adult identified as the potential source of the imbalance.

Step 5: Put the plan into action. In doing this, be sure the child for whom the plan has been written fully understands and embraces the plan (if appropriate). Begin charting the frequency of the targeted behavior or symptom on the first day of the plan, and continue charting the number of occurrences daily. Keep the plan in a convenient place for both you and the child, respecting the child's need for confidentiality.

Step 6: Chart the frequency of the targeted behavior for one week. Watch the pattern that evolves relative to the baseline frequency (number of behaviors before implementing the plan). If there is a decrease in the frequency of behaviors from the baseline number of behaviors, continue the current plan until the child's behavior reaches a point of balance (in an acceptable range compared to other children of similar age).

Step 7: If the plan is successful, celebrate with the child. Note if any other behaviors in the child have changed as a result of rebalancing. It is a common occurrence that once a greater degree of balance has been reached in one area, balance is reestablished in other areas of functioning as well.

If your plan has not been successful, consider other options or strategies, or consider consulting a specialist who may have more information regarding options for bringing the targeted behavior into balance.

Up until the time a child enters school or a childcare program, it is the parent's responsibility to identify and work with the behaviors of the child. Once the child becomes involved with other adults in a childcare setting, preschool, or school setting, this process often becomes a collaborative process among the adults living and working with the child needing support. Cooperative efforts among these adults are in the best interest of the child.

Chapter 7

Mental Symptoms and Sources Associated with Learning

If a child is learning at a rate consistent with the expectation for his or her age and uniqueness, one can assume that the internal functions of the child and the external learning conditions are in sync with each other. However, if a child is not progressing within an appropriate age range in one or more areas of development or learning, an adult should begin monitoring the situation. To do this, it is necessary to be aware of what constitutes a significant discrepancy in performance with respect to age. The Gesell Institute of Human Development in New Haven, Connecticut, considers a range within plus or minus six months for a particular developmental behavior to be appropriate for younger children. For school-age children, this range of expectation varies among school districts and is most often based on standard scores.

A child generally gives the first clue when an imbalance is emerging. The clue usually lies in either physical or emotional symptoms, social behaviors, or the child's attitude toward certain types of learning. For a young child, the clue can be observed as the child explores his or her environment, practices large and small motor skills, and develops language skills. Before a child's language skills develop, adults need to rely on interpreting what certain behaviors mean. At these younger ages, one must observe not only the most obvious behaviors but also the more subtle, nonverbal behaviors of facial expressions and body language. As a child develops language skills, it is important to talk with him or her about what is happening. To make this a more productive process, children should be taught feeling words and problem-solving skills as soon as appropriate for their age and language skills.

As children progress in school, issues may surface in the academic areas of reading, math, writing, and/or language. Minimally, all tasks in these areas require attention, concentration, memory, language and small motor skills, seeing relationships, and learning in a social context.

Observing a child in the context in which the behavior occurs is key to addressing a problem. Following are some guidelines:

- Observe the child in a number of different situations, such as doing a task alone, doing a task with peers, or doing a task with an adult. Note the situation/s in which the child performs best.

Creating Balance in Children's Lives

- Put aside all judgment and assumption, and just watch and listen to what the child is doing and saying.

- Jot down what you see and hear.

- Pay close attention to the behavior of the child, especially watching for gestures, facial expressions, and other nonverbal body language.

- Listen to the child's comments about the task and about himself or herself while doing the task.

- Note the ease with which the child engages in the task, any difficulties the child has in doing the task, and any behaviors such as becoming aggressive, giving up, or walking away from the task.

- Observe and record the child's behavior several times to determine the consistency/inconsistency of the behavior and to look for any common patterns among several observations.

- Summarize your observations.

If you and/or others with whom you collaborate determine that a problem exists, begin to look for possible sources. During this process, always remember to look for sources within the child and within all environments in which a child participates. Some imbalances occur as a result of something going on internally with a child, some occur as a result of what is happening in the environment, and some occur as a result of both. Determining the source/s is crucial in planning how to correct an imbalance. If, for example, a child is in a state of imbalance due to parental and/or educational expectations, or a mismatch exists between the curriculum and the child, attempting to change something within the child will be unsuccessful. In identifying the potential source/s of the imbalance, consideration should be given to:

- the difficulty of the task relative to the child's readiness to learn the skills required to do the task

- whether the child has learned the prerequisite skills necessary for learning the skills of the targeted task

- whether the child has the visual abilities, eye/hand coordination, and language processing abilities to do the task

- whether the child has any physical impairments that might interfere with learning the skills required for the task

- whether the emotional climate in which the task is presented is somehow threatening to the child

- any trauma or changes in the child's environment that may be causing the child considerable emotional stress

- the motivation of the child to learn

Sometimes additional information is needed about the child and the environment where the imbalance is occurring before deciding on a plan of action. If this is the case, then the adult/s involved must determine what additional information is needed, and how and where to get the information. When all the information has been gathered, identify the potential source of the imbalance, and take the actions listed in steps three through seven provided in this chapter on pages 83 and 84.

Emotional/Social Symptoms and Sources

The emotional development of children plays a vital part in how they feel about themselves, their general state of well-being, how they interact with others, and how they interact with the learning process. Positive emotions, such as joy, love, and feeling nurtured, support the state of balance desired for the body and mind to interact well with others and achieve optimal learning performance. Negative emotions such as fear, anger, and frustration activate a survival mode in the nervous system that persists until the negative emotions are diffused or released. The prolonged stress caused by negative emotions compromises the body's immune system and keeps the body in a continuous state of anxiety, a state of imbalance. When this happens, children need the assistance of adults to bring them back into a state of emotional balance. To decide when help is necessary, adults need to be aware of the behaviors associated with emotional/social imbalance. In the process of identifying these behaviors, keep in mind:

Creating Balance in Children's Lives

- the age of the child (as what is appropriate for a young child is very different from what is appropriate for an adolescent)

- the child's cultural background (as different cultures often have different expectations and norms for behavior)

- the environment/s in which the imbalance occurs

Most children exhibit a wide variety of emotions in their day-to-day lives. It is when a negative emotion or behavior is excessive that it becomes a concern and a potential indicator of imbalance. Remedial action should be taken if a child:

- cries frequently and out of context for the situation

- is very fearful of new situations and new people

- carries a chip on his or her shoulder or conveys a pervasive negative attitude

- destroys property on a regular basis

- worries more than others (about being alone, losing a loved one, going to school)

- has quick, drastic mood changes, i.e., from happy to sad, loving to angry, helpful to hurtful, etc.

- has frequent, uncontrollable temper tantrums or outbursts

- is easily frustrated in efforts and/or not satisfied with outcomes

- displays a pervasive mood of hopelessness

- is cruel to animals and/or other people

- bullies others and/or fights constantly

- cannot make or keep friends

- blames others for anything bad that happens

To determine if one or more of these behaviors (or any other behavior) is excessive, a baseline frequency chart can be made. (See Figure 7.1.) If the identified behavior is frequent enough and of an intensity that interferes with the child's well-being and/or the well-being of others, a plan to change the behavior (correct the imbalance) should be put into action. (See steps three through seven provided in this chapter on pages 83 and 84.)

Guidelines for Rebalancing

The guidelines offered below are directed toward the adult responsible for helping a child rebalance and should facilitate the success of this endeavor.

In reviewing these guidelines, choose those that are appropriate for the circumstance, and add others that will facilitate the process of change.

1. Regardless of your relationship to the child (parent, childcare provider, educator), it is important that you take as objective a view as possible toward the behavior being targeted. It is easy to get caught up in your own emotions, which can prevent you from seeing all aspects of the problem.

2. As much as possible, attempt to see the issues involved from the child's point of view in addition to your own point of view. If age appropriate, ask the child for his or her thoughts and feelings about the targeted behavior.

3. Remember to separate the behavior from the child. You want to find the cause for the behavior and correct whatever is contributing to it, not the child. The child needs to know that it is his or her behavior that needs to be changed and that he or she is still loved.

4. As you work with the identified behavior, be careful not to get into a position of overcare (caring so much you lose a reasoned perspective) or get discouraged and withdraw from trying to correct the imbalance.

5. If unanswered questions and concerns surface, consult others about identifying the source of the imbalance or determining options, and then set a course of action.

6. Once a plan of action is initiated, chart the child's progress over a sufficient period of time. Although immediate change is possible, it usually takes a while. As long as progress is being made, continue the plan of action. If progress is not made, you need to look for another source of the imbalance and/or devise a new plan of action.

7. Generally, it is advisable to rule out any physical and/or cognitive sources associated with learning before looking for emotional sources. Physical and cognitive imbalances can both trigger behaviors that appear to be of an emotional nature. And, of course, an emotional imbalance can trigger physical symptoms and learning difficulties. All of these levels are interconnected. However, the physical level gives us a more objective place with which to start. As one is assessing the situation, the behavior may also need to be addressed at the level where the symptoms occur. For example, if a child has a learning difficulty that is the result of nutritional problems, both aspects of the situation should be addressed. Likewise, if a child has an emotional problem that is the result of a learning difficulty, both of these areas require a plan of action.

It is evident that the symptoms and sources of imbalance in children's lives can be very complex, but understanding them is crucial to our children's future and our own. Our approach must be holistic in order to achieve the desired balance. The ideas presented here are but the beginning of an ever-evolving way of living and working with children.

The next chapter provides a glimpse of what children say about their own sense of peace, another word for balance, and how children themselves say they can bring peace into their lives.

Key Points of Chapter 7

- It is best ameliorate or eliminate sources of stress before related symptoms and behaviors appear in children, but sometimes we are not aware of the stress until we see the symptoms. Then care must be taken to discover and ameliorate or eliminate the

Chapter 7

source/s so that relationships, learning, and well-being are not compromised.

- Physical imbalances may be revealed in symptoms such as insufficient or excessive energy, frequent colds and other illnesses, general lethargy, problems breathing, irritability, eating problems, sleeping problems, frequent headaches, or frequent stomachaches.

- Mental imbalances related to learning can show up as problems with attention, concentration, memory, language, small motor skills, seeing relationships, and learning in a social context. To determine if a problem really exists, first consider what can be expected of the child given his or her age (within a range of plus or minus six months for younger children).

- Emotional/social imbalances can negatively affect a child's general state of well-being, how the child interacts with others, and how he or she interacts with the learning process. Prolonged stress caused by negative emotions compromises the body's immune system and keeps the body in a continuous state of anxiety, or imbalance, which, in turn, compromises learning and behavior.

- To address the imbalance, document the frequency of the symptom or behavior and determine possible sources. Create and implement an action plan to address the most likely source, enlisting the child's cooperation. Continue documenting the symptom or behavior to see if progress is being made. When progress is made, celebrate with the child.

Notes

CHAPTER 8

THE WISDOM OF CHILDREN

"Peace is a wonderful thing that comes from the heart."

A child

What parent or teacher has not been awed by the intuitive wisdom that can come from children? With this thought in mind, the authors surveyed about 300 five- through thirteen-year-old children in the early '90s in several public schools in the Minneapolis, Minnesota, area. We asked them questions about peace, a term they could relate to better than balance. Their answers give us clues as to what adults can provide for children to help them achieve a peaceful (balanced) sense of well-being.

From "the Mouths of Babes"

We asked the children the following questions:

- What do you think of when you think of peace?
- Where does peace come from?
- When do you feel peaceful?
- How can you help yourself feel more peaceful?
- How do you feel when you feel peaceful?

Their answers confirm that balance is a complex interaction between the body, mind, heart, and spirit. In other words, a balanced, peaceful state of being involves physical, psychological, emotional/social, and spiritual aspects of oneself. Following is what the children had to say.

Thinking of Peace

When they thought of peace, children thought of such qualities as: "contentment," "understanding," "gentleness," "happiness," "calmness," "kindness," "freedom," "caring," and "respect," as well as "joy and being thankful for what you have." They wrote of "feeling good about yourself and not putting others down," "friends that care about you and like you for who you are," "people loving each other," "hugs," and "fun." Their ideas ranged from "a nice relaxing time" to "being at one with yourself." (No, we are not making these up!)

Creating Balance in Children's Lives

The Source of Peace

When asked where peace comes from, one child said, "Peace is a wonderful thing that comes from the heart." Other children thought that peace comes from "the mind and the spirit," "your soul," "within yourself," and "thinking about peace." They also mentioned "love for each other," "being helpful and honest," "everybody's cooperation in the world," "friends and family," and "God."

Helping Themselves

Self-esteem was a dominant thread weaving through the children's responses. Some of the ways they felt they could help themselves be more peaceful were: "Being proud of myself," "telling myself I'm neat and creative," "solving problems well and not hurting anyone else or ME," "staying the way I am and not letting anyone else tell me what to do," and "trying to help myself feel good about me."

Children also said they could help themselves be more peaceful by: "not getting mad at myself," "trying not to worry," "using mind control to calm myself down," "not letting problems get to me," "not getting so angry," and "not being jealous of anyone or hating anyone." From a more positive perspective, they thought they could be more peaceful by: "relaxing and trying to get everything out of my mind," "sharing my feelings with others," "being alone praying to God," and "taking more time for myself." When they were stressed out and felt like "just sometimes taking a break from all the confusion" or "just acting normal," they might have taken this child's advice: "Stop two, breathe two, go take a walk."

Nature and Animals

Many of the children wrote about nature and animals in connection with peace. This approach involves "people and animals living together in harmony." It means enjoying "God's nature," which includes "butterflies," "bunnies," "puppies," "a sunset and flowers in the middle of nowhere," "prairie with green grass," "sun and a stream," the "ocean" and "stars." It involves: "playing with my dog outside," "riding horseback," "visiting my rats," "fishing," and "sitting on the dock with my feet in the water, watching boats go by and listening to the birds and the wind." One child felt peaceful when he could "help with the environment," another when "gardening on a peaceful morning," and others when "sitting outside and watching the clouds and animals," and "sitting on this big rock down by our lake in the early evening."

Chapter 8

Music and Dancing

A kindergarten boy said he felt peaceful when "I'm taking a bubble bath with my music on," and another child said when "I listen to my music and I can be myself." Other musical strategies were "playing the piano" and "singing." One of the children said she felt peaceful "when I dance, because I feel good knowing that dancing is something I can do."

Writing, Reading, and Drawing

One child said peace brought to mind "when I am alone and jotting down a day in my diary." Another mentioned "being in a quiet area at home writing down all my good thoughts about my family, friends, and the world." Others said "reading a good book," being "alone writing or reading," and "drawing."

Loving and Sharing

At a deep level, children understand the emotional/social aspects of balance and peace. They said they felt peaceful when: "I am loving myself and others are loving me," "my Dad's family gets together and plays poker, tag, and hide-and-seek," "I am happy and loved," and "me and my whole family are watching a movie together at my grandma's house." Others said they felt peaceful when: "I know somebody cares about me," "I'm sharing things and laughing," and "I'm sitting with mom and dad watching the rain." They knew they could help themselves be more peaceful by "giving mom and dad flowers," "learning to share with my brother," "loving and caring about somebody," "being kind to others," "loving someone who is blind," and "sometimes not picking on others at school." One child summed it up by stating that "unconditionally loving and supporting everyone" was the answer.

The End Results

When they felt peaceful, children said they felt: "good, and I can think more clearly," "able to do things without being bothered," "proud," "friendly," "satisfied," "joyful," and "glad I'm alive." They felt "great," "humble," "helpful," "calm," and "adventurous." Others felt "loved," "good inside," and "like I'm in a whole different world." One wrote that she felt "very relaxed and I feel like a feather," and another felt "gentle like a sleeping swan." An eighth-grade boy in a group of emotionally disturbed

Creating Balance in Children's Lives

children wrote that when he felt peaceful, he felt "fancy-free, spiritual, special, immortal."

How Adults Can Help

By the beautiful and insightful expressions above, we can see that feeling balanced and peaceful is well worth what it takes to achieve—for both children and adults. The children's statements also help us understand the kinds of experiences that adults can provide in order to facilitate balance and peace in children's lives. A good beginning is to be a role model of the qualities mentioned. Then help children achieve a balance between alone time and time with family and friends, as well as a balance between different types of activities. Make sure children have access to nature and animals as well as good books and music. Give them a sense of the spiritual in their lives. Help them solve problems, share their feelings, care about others, and love themselves.

The next chapter presents many more specific options for creating balance in children's lives. If you feel yourself becoming overwhelmed by the possibilities, just "stop two, breathe two, go take a walk." And all will be well.

Key Points of Chapter 8

- Asking children what they think can result in answers of considerable depth that may provide significant insight to the adults who work and live with those children.

- Children connected peace with positive qualities such as contentment, calmness, clarity of mind, and respect, as well as with solving problems well and doing things they loved. When they thought of peace, they thought of family, friends, and God.

- Children said that peace comes from the mind, the heart, and the spirit.

- They said that some of the ways they could help themselves be more peaceful were to try not to think negatively, love more, share their feelings, and relax.

Chapter 8

- Children connected peace with animals and nature as well as music and the arts and reading.

- When children felt peaceful, they felt happy, friendly, helpful, and loved, and they could think more clearly.

- Adults can help children feel more peaceful, or balanced, by providing the kinds of experiences the children mentioned, encouraging the qualities the children connected with peace, and being role models of peace and balance.

Notes

CHAPTER 9

OPTIONS FOR PREVENTING AND CORRECTING IMBALANCES

"With both heart and mind, we can build caring communities, design schools that develop children's wisdom and emotional strength along with their intellect and physical strength, and operate institutions with balance, intelligence, and appreciation for people and the environment."

Doc Childre *(Freeze-Frame: Fast Action Stress Relief)*

Our goal for all children is to provide conditions and experiences that will encourage and ensure children's optimal health, learning abilities, and emotional, social, and spiritual growth. This requires that we meet each child's physiological and growth needs within an environment that supports these needs in a balanced way. (Refer to the Wheel of Balance, page 70.) This chapter begins with a summary of physiological and growth needs and supportive environmental conditions. Then, options are presented that can be used to help prevent and correct imbalances in children.

Needs and Conditions

Note that although our focus here is on children, the following needs and conditions are universal for all human beings. Some may seem obvious, but sadly, they are not always met.

Physiological Needs

- a sufficient amount of clean air
- a sufficient intake of pure water
- sufficient natural (full-spectrum) light
- nutrients that are growth-enhancing and life-sustaining
- adequate amounts and quality of relaxation and sleep time

Creating Balance in Children's Lives

- sufficient movement to provide the body with exercise and opportunities for motor development and sensory integration
- a safe, comfortable shelter in which to live
- adequate clothing to protect a child's body under a variety of conditions

Growth Needs

- stimulation of the five outer senses
- stimulation of inner senses such as intuition and creativity
- emotional connections
- a sense of belonging (being a part of a family, neighborhood, school, or other group)
- a connection with the arts
- a connection with nature and animals
- a sense of the sacred

Environmental Conditions

- a safe (physical and psychological) environment in which to live, play, and work
- sufficient time to meet the needs in all four quadrants (physical, mental, emotional/social, spiritual)
- sufficient space in which to be and move
- a comfortable temperature in which to live and work and/or appropriate clothing for the child's level of comfort
- adequate lighting for ease of function (for children, this means in play, home, and school environments)

- a balanced level of sound that will not cause harm to a child's hearing and cause stress to the body

- known boundaries and limits

- presence of supportive and caring adults

- an environment free of harmful chemicals and pesticides or where any toxic substances are well out of reach

The more these needs and conditions are met for children, the greater the likelihood they will be in an overall state of balance, which then supports their health, learning, and behavior. When these factors are supported, children are more likely to have better relationships and the ability to adapt to the demands of their environments in a balanced way.

Options for Enhancing or Creating Balance

When indicators such as symptoms of discomfort, health problems, learning difficulties, and behavioral difficulties occur, adults need to determine which of the above needs are not being met and choose options for rebalancing the child's state of being. The options outlined in this chapter are choices for creating more balance in children's lives, preventing as many imbalances as possible, and correcting imbalances when they occur. A first step is to look at the lifestyles that we, as adults, have created for children.

Lifestyle

Lifestyle covers many areas and serves as the foundation for creating balance in children's lives. The fast pace of many lifestyles in America contributes to:

- a lack of balance between scheduled time and unscheduled time

- too many fast-food meals

- a lack of quality time between adults and children

- insufficient time to get adequate exercise

Creating Balance in Children's Lives

- insufficient time for relaxation

- a quest for "quick fixes," such as drugs, when something goes wrong

As a part of this lifestyle pattern, children from very young ages are scheduled for much of the day, whether it is in childcare situations, school, or extra activities. For many children, this continuous "doing" does not allow for sufficient downtime, time for imaginative and creative activities, or spontaneous play. Over time, these factors cause stress on the Dynamic Trio, which manifests in health, learning, and/or behavioral difficulties. An evaluation of lifestyle, childcare situations, and various activity schedules is a way to start addressing the issue of balance in children's lives. Once potential sources of imbalance are recognized in any of these areas, options and changes can be considered. As a part of this evaluation process, it is crucial for parents to look at what they are feeding their families and for schools to evaluate the nutrition of the school lunches they provide.

Nutrition

Parents initially control the food that comes into the house and set the example for "good" or "bad" eating habits in the home. Since examples are more powerful than words for children, setting a good example for children at the beginning of their lives is essential for their future eating habits. Schools need to support healthy eating habits by evaluating their lunch programs (now often consisting of "fast food" and processed foods), changing them where necessary. They can also explore ways to incorporate learning about nutrition into their curricula for all ages.

All of the cells in the body and brain need proper nutrition to carry out their functions. We are familiar with the fact that the body needs nutrients to grow, develop, maintain health, and have an adequate supply of energy to participate in life. Studies that began about 15 years ago have confirmed the fact that there is a relationship between what children eat and how they think, act, and learn. In January of 2003, Appleton (Wisconsin) Central Alternative High School was heralded on ABC's "Good Morning America" for getting rid of vending machines and fast-food burgers in exchange for a whole-food menu developed by Natural Ovens Bakery out of Manitowoc, Wisconsin. It was reported that since this initiative began in 1997, grades have gone up, truancy is less frequent, and teachers marvel at the radical improvement in student behavior. The evidence is clear that diet is a crucial part of children's

Chapter 9

learning and behavior. It is also clear that diets consisting of fast foods, highly processed foods, excess sugar, and caffeinated beverages do not support optimal learning and behavior. Another encouraging fact is that we now know more about nutrition and how various nutrients interact with the body and the brain.

Healthy Diets for Children

Nutritionists and scientists now generally agree that a healthy diet to support bone and muscle growth and learning should include a daily intake of proteins, complex carbohydrates, unsaturated fats, and fiber. Specific foods that are good for the brain include: nuts, lean meats, salmon, leafy green vegetables, and fresh fruits (Connors).

In planning a healthy diet for children, it is important to remember that children's nutritional needs change from birth through adolescence. For example, children need more unsaturated fats in their diet the first few years of their lives. It is also important to keep in mind that whole grains are a better source of nutrients than highly processed grains, fresh vegetables contain more nutrients than frozen or canned vegetables, and fresh fruits are the best source of fruit for children. A general rule to follow when you buy fruits and vegetables is that the closer you are to where they were grown and the closer the food is to its natural form, the higher the value of the nutrients in the food will be.

All children (and adults) need to start out their day with a healthy breakfast consisting of protein and complex carbohydrates. Some children skip breakfast because they are not hungry or don't allow the time needed. The children who do this often have more trouble concentrating and less speed and accuracy in retrieving information from memory—two very necessary components of learning. In addition, a study by the Harvard Medical School found that skipping breakfast doubles the risk of developing obesity and insulin resistance.

Children need a healthy lunch to continue learning well through the afternoon. In the case where a school serves a menu consisting of chicken nuggets and other highly processed food, it is better for children to bring their own lunch. Loading up on sweets at either breakfast or lunch gives children a surge of energy followed by a lowering of blood-sugar levels, which results in little fuel being available for learning. It is beyond the scope of this book to provide the specifics of healthy eating, but many good resources provide this information. In looking for resources on nutrition, be sure the focus is on children's nutrition rather

Creating Balance in Children's Lives

than adult nutrition. A few of these resources are listed in the Resources section in the back of this book.

Quality of Food

There are many concerns regarding the quality of the food we ingest these days. Over-processing, the extensive use of hydrogenated oils, and high sugar and salt contents lower food quality. In addition, concern is increasing over the amount of residues that many foods contain from the use of pesticides and chemical fertilizers in growing food and the use of preservatives in storing food.

The nutritional value of our food has been declining. According to the National Academy of Science, "It now takes twice as many vegetables to get the daily requirement of many vitamins and minerals compared to 1975!" This statement is based on the latest food tables released by the U.S. Department of Agriculture, showing the nutritional content of fruits and vegetables. For example:

- spinach: Vitamin C content is down 45 percent.
- cauliflower: Vitamin C content is down 40 percent.
- broccoli: Calcium content is down 50 percent.
- corn: Calcium is down 78 percent, vitamin C is down 41 percent, vitamin A is down 29 percent, and magnesium is down 22 percent.
- collards: Vitamin A content is down 42 percent, potassium is down 58 percent, and magnesium is down 84 percent.

The implication of this trend is that both children and adults need to eat more of these foods to get the same amount of nutrients as before, or they need to take daily vitamin and mineral supplements. Another option to consider is to change from eating conventionally grown food to organically grown food as much as possible given the availability of organic foods and the family budget.

Food quality is also decreased by the use of a variety of preservatives (such as MSG) and dyes used in many of the food products we consume. Aspartame, a popular synthetic sugar, is used in many of our diet and low-calorie beverages and other food products. Concern is increasing over the use of this product for people of any age. In his book, *Aspartame Disease,* H. J. Roberts, M.D., documents results from reports of his patients and a survey he conducted on the effects of aspartame. He raises several concerns about the use of this synthetic sweetener (appearing under the brand names of a few well-known artificial sweeteners) in food products and beverages. His work is based on over 1,000 cases where adverse effects from the use of artificial sweeteners have been reported. Other physicians and health practitioners are also raising questions regarding the potential neurotoxic effects of aspartame on children and adults. Children are especially vulnerable to the harmful effects of neurotoxins, as their nervous systems are still developing.

Given this information, it is in the best interests of all children (and adults) to use natural sweeteners, such as stevia or Sucanat® (SUgar CAne NATurally), as much as possible, at least until further research confirms or clears the potential for adverse effects with aspartame. It is especially important to pursue this course when behavior, learning, and/or health problems exist.

As a starting point, adults can become more aware of the substances in food products by reading labels so they can buy wisely. The next step is to check out what the risks are if one ingests aspartame, MSG, excess sugar, food dyes, etc. on a regular basis. Some sources of information regarding these ingredients are the World Natural Health Organization, the Environmental Protection Agency, the National Institutes of Health, and the Greater Boston Physicians for Social Responsibility organization.

Nutrition as Treatment

Nutrition is becoming more widely accepted as a treatment option for learning and behavior problems. Many successful cases have been reported in which a change of diet resulted in the decrease or elimination of learning and attention problems and improved behavior. It is advisable in all cases when a child's health, learning, or behavior is compromised to determine if diet is the primary or contributing factor. Good sources of information on this topic include Jacqueline Stordy's book, *The LCP Solution,* and the chapter on nutrition in Carla Hannaford's book *Smart Moves.* (See Resources.)

Creating Balance in Children's Lives

Movement

Children need to move! Movement not only helps children's sensory-motor development, but it also helps to circulate oxygen and nutrients to all parts of the Dynamic Trio, to balance the right and left hemispheres of the brain for greater learning, and to bring a greater sense of overall balance to the body. Movement is becoming more and more important in these times of excessive TV watching, video-game playing, and computer use.

Movement can come in many forms, such as participating in individual and group sports, spontaneous play, walking, running, or dancing. Many Westerners have taken up Eastern forms of exercise, such as yoga, tai chi, karate, and tae kwon do. Another option is Brain Gym®, a specific series of movements created to balance the body for improved motor coordination, learning, and behavior. More about Brain Gym, yoga, and tai chi follows.

Brain Gym, yoga, and tai chi as forms of movement are appropriate for groups of school children, families, and individual practice. They also have been well established for a number of years, and documented research exists as to their benefits. All these forms of movement are appropriate for children from about age three and up and all adults regardless of age.

Brain Gym

Brain Gym International is a worldwide network specializing in research and applied programs of physical movement to enhance learning in all areas. Using the Brain Gym movements on a regular basis has been found to bring about improvements in concentration, memory, reading, organization skills, language and number skills, writing, speaking, athletic performance, and overall health. Improvement in these areas often results in improved overall behavior, an increase in self-confidence, and a decrease in anxiety.

Brain Gym activities have been used successfully with children who have learning difficulties, including attention and concentration problems. Relative to ADD or ADHD, it can be a viable alternative to the use of drugs. Brain Gym International has a comprehensive Web site and several excellent books that parents and educators can use to introduce and incorporate these movements into children's lives. (These references and others mentioned in this chapter are listed in the

Chapter 9

Resources section of this book.) Throughout the world, trainers are available to help interested people get started. Classrooms that use these movements on a regular basis have seen benefits in the learning and behavior of their students.

Yoga

Tara Guber and Leah Kalsih have developed a comprehensive, 36-week yoga education program (Yoga Ed.™), encompassing three developmental levels: grades K-2, 3-5, and 6-8. This program meets both the California and the National Physical Education Standards. According to the developers, the program "enhances concentration, listening readiness, stress reduction, behavioral skills, physical health and emotional stability in children." Their primary purpose as an organization is to create and distribute yoga-based education programs and materials to schools nationwide as well as train both yoga and classroom teachers in the Yoga Ed. philosophy and method. This program was first implemented at The Accelerated School (TAS) in South Central Los Angeles. At this school, all of the students participate in Yoga Ed. twice a week as part of the Physical Education program. The program has had positive effects for individual students as well as for the overall climate of the school. Yoga Ed. is available for all schools, grades K-8.

Yoga for the Special Child™ is a comprehensive program of yoga specifically designed to enhance the natural development of children with special needs. It is a style of yoga that is gentle and therapeutic. As such, it is considered safe for babies and children with Down's syndrome, cerebral palsy, autism, and other developmental disabilities. The methods used have also provided effective treatment for children diagnosed with ADD, ADHD, and LD. This yoga program includes an integrated series of balanced yoga poses to increase body awareness, strength, and flexibility, specialized breathing exercises, and relaxation techniques to improve concentration and reduce hyperactivity. It also has an early intervention program to assure the healthy early development of infants and toddlers. Sonia Sumar, the renowned yoga therapist and author who developed these methods, has been working with children for more than 25 years and has written a book titled *Yoga for the Special Child*.

Creating Balance in Children's Lives

Tai Chi

Tai chi is an ancient form of movement that originated in China. Adults in the United States have been practicing tai chi for many years, and now American children are beginning to take up the practice. Children especially enjoy the tai chi movements that are based on animal behaviors and movements. As with yoga, tai chi improves circulation, body strength and flexibility, attention, balance, and overall health. A book on tai chi for children is listed in the Resources section. As the benefits of tai chi for health, balance, and learning become better known, we should see an increase in the number of related books and the teaching of this form of movement in school settings.

It has been reliably demonstrated that movement is critical to a child's state of balance, health, learning, and behavior. Listed here are but a few types of movement activities available to children. Adults need to explore the options and then decide on a course of action that will bring more movement into children's lives. This is especially critical now that more pressure is being put on our educational systems to focus on academics at the expense of the arts and physical activities. Without a balance of activities, the learning and behavior of children will be further compromised. The resulting increase in problems could lead to an even greater use of drugs rather than the use of natural means to try to correct imbalances in children.

Music

Music is a universal language that can inspire, calm, and energize the minds and bodies of all who listen to or participate in creating it. It also activates many different parts of the brain, which helps more of the brain's functions to be involved in creating and thinking and facilitates a greater degree of balance between the left and right hemispheres of the brain. However, to achieve the benefits of enhanced learning, memory, and energy, it is necessary to be aware of the type and volume of music and choose it appropriately.

We have learned much about the effects of music through the work of the Bulgarian physician Georgi Lozanov and his team, the French physician Alfred Tomatis, contemporary Superlearning composer and music therapist, Janalea Hoffman, and others. We now know that music with a tempo of about 60-70 beats a minute and a sound frequency of approximately 5,000 to 8,000 cycles per second helps create the condition referred to as relaxed body, alert mind. This is a state in which the heart beats at a healthy rhythm (about 60 beats a minute) and the brainwave patterns of beta and alpha are in a balanced, alert state, an ideal state for optimal accomplishment of the mind. In this state of calmness, the body functions more efficiently on less energy, which makes more energy available to the brain. In his work with children and adults, Tomatis found the music of Mozart was richest in these ultrahigh frequencies. The music of other composers, such as Vivaldi and Bach, has been used for accelerating learning in various Superlearning programs or courses. In analyzing the effectiveness of different tempos of music for learning, researchers found that it was the slow parts of Baroque concertos, with tempos of about 60 beats a minute, that increased learning. For a list of slow Baroque music pieces, 60-beats-a-minute contemporary music selections, and sources for this music, see the book *Superlearning 2000,* listed in the Resources section.

Music therapy has been found to be an effective aid to reducing stress and facilitating the healing of various illnesses of the body and mental conditions in children and adults. Music has been used as an adjunct to medicine for thousands of years. A more formalized approach to its use in hospitals began in World War II, when U.S. Veteran Administration hospitals began to use music to help treat soldiers suffering from shell shock. Music therapy is now used in medical hospitals, rehabilitation centers, daycare treatment centers, community mental health centers, and many other settings to help reduce stress, calm people, and improve mental and physical health. As an example, Beth Israel's (NY) neonatal intensive care unit found that one hour of music every day helps babies "eat more, sleep more, and gain more weight."

Just as some frequencies of sound balance and energize the mind and body, some frequencies deplete them. These are the low-frequency sounds, such as noise from traffic, airports, and construction sites. It has been found that some of the low, pounding sounds in rock music are also "brain drain" sounds. Over time, noise pollution, turning up the bass, and listening to music containing many low-frequency sounds can cause a hearing impairment. When this happens, the ear is less able to hear the energizing high-frequency sounds, as hearing impairment reduces the range of frequencies that can be heard by both children and adults. This has become an increasing concern in our culture as the number of hearing impairments has continued to rise over the last decade. This trend will no doubt continue until we, as adults, become aware of the effects of music and sound, learn what we can do about them, and take action to help bring music and sound that supports balance into

Creating Balance in Children's Lives

children's lives and our own. Following are steps we can begin to take along these lines:

- Explore the effects of music by listening to different types of music while engaging in a variety of activities and downtime to determine the effects of the music on our feelings and actions during these periods of time. It is important to include "live" music along with recorded music. It is especially important for children to hear live music to develop their acuity for hearing high-frequency sounds, because live music is a better source of these sounds than digitalized music.

- Apply this same process to the children in our lives by asking for feedback from the child, when appropriate, and by observing the behaviors of the child.

- Acquaint ourselves with the effect of music on adults and on children through reading books on the subject, searching the Internet, and talking with others who are knowledgeable about the subject. The books *The Mozart Effect* and *The Mozart Effect for Children* by Don Campbell and several chapters in *Superlearning 2000* explain the effects of music and list many musical selections that are appropriate for various age groups of children.

- Be aware of the music volume that is most resonant to (comfortable for) the mind and body.

- Stay abreast of the new information emerging regarding the use and effects of music and how we can create healthy sound environments for children and adults.

- Use music in a variety of ways with children from birth through adolescence. Music Together® and Kindermusik® are nationally available music programs that are especially designed for children from birth through five years of age. Listening to music, doing movements to music, and playing different instruments all help children to feel the rhythm of music, hear the tonal quality of music, and sense the organized patterns of music. Such experiences are important for the growth and development of children, because they enhance brain functions and memory and help the mind and body to reduce stress.

Auditory stimulation programs based on incorporating music and sound have been successful in bringing greater balance into the lives of children who have been identified as having one or more learning problems. These programs are tailored to the needs of the individual child. They have helped children who have language, reading, and attention problems, children with the diagnosis of autism, and others who are experiencing a variety of challenges. Currently, most of these programs, such as the Tomatis Method, require parents to work within a clinic setting rather than a school setting. Even though this may be more difficult in terms of effort and cost, it is worthwhile for children who can benefit from this type of intervention.

Light and Color

Natural light contains the full spectrum of colors. This includes every variation of the basic colors we see so beautifully displayed in rainbows: red, orange, yellow, green, blue, indigo, and violet. Since colors are forms of energy, they each have characteristic frequencies at which they vibrate. Our bodies and brains "tune in" to these frequencies to help maintain a state of dynamic balance that influences our physical health and our emotional and mental states. When we are deprived of natural light and/or the frequencies of the full spectrum of colors, our health, moods, and mental capacities are negatively affected. People who live in areas where there are fewer daylight hours or many gray days during certain times of the year are especially at risk for the condition termed Seasonal Affective Disorder (SAD). This condition can be corrected or lessened by bringing more natural light into indoor environments in the form of full-spectrum lighting. This kind of lighting is the closest match to sunlight, and it contains the full range of the basic colors. Regular fluorescent bulbs and incandescent bulbs, the two types of artificial light normally used indoors, contain only some of the colors of the spectrum.

Research by Dr. John Ott, a photobiologist, and others has established the fact that humans need to get an ample supply of natural light on a regular basis. He first demonstrated the importance of this in 1973, when he conducted a study using four windowless classrooms of first graders in the state of Florida. For purposes of the study, full-spectrum fluorescent lighting replaced the standard cool-white fluorescent lighting in two of the four classrooms. After one month, it was reported that behavior, class performance, and overall achievement improved significantly in the two classrooms with full-spectrum lighting compared to the two with standard fluorescent lighting. Also reported was the fact

Creating Balance in Children's Lives

that several learning-disabled children in the full-spectrum classrooms who had extreme hyperactivity calmed down and seemed to overcome some of their learning problems. Since 1973, several other studies concerned with the effect of light quality on children's behavior and performance have reported similar results. Such studies have also been conducted in workplaces. The results of these studies report that full-spectrum lighting lowered the stress on the nervous system and reduced the number of absences, thus increasing work performance.

In addition to the quality of light emitted by full-spectrum lighting compared to artificial lighting, it is important to note that cool-white fluorescent lights produce a constant humming sound. For children and adults who have a sensitivity to sound, this can become an additional source of stress on their bodies and minds.

The benefits of full-spectrum lighting are sufficiently documented that this type of lighting definitely should be considered to help bring more balance into all of our lives.

Using Color Practically

Color surrounds us 24 hours a day. It surrounds us in the clothes we wear, the food we eat, the colors of nature, and the colors that are used in our homes, schools, workplaces, and other environments. Often we have no choice about the colors that surround us. However, in many circumstances we can choose the color or colors that will serve our purposes. Our bodies and minds are affected in certain ways by the specific vibrations of each color. Therefore, it pays to become aware of which colors energize us, which deplete our energies, which make us feel calm, and so on. Then we can use colors wisely to support children's (and our own) overall state of balance.

The frequencies of colors and their various effects on the human body have been well established by scientists and practitioners who use color to facilitate learning, change behavior, or use color therapeutically for healing purposes. Considering the basic colors of the rainbow, the red end of the spectrum is energizing, while the blue end of the spectrum is restorative. The color green, in the middle of the spectrum, is associated with the qualities of balance and harmony. The frequencies of red, orange, and yellow stimulate, activate, motivate, and warm the receiver, whereas the frequencies of blue, indigo, and violet calm, sooth, and cool. With these basic qualities of the color spectrum in mind, we can begin to consciously choose colors of clothing and colors for the indoor environment to suit different purposes.

For parents, this means guiding children in the choice of colors they wear and carefully choosing the colors in the areas where they play and sleep. For example, red and/or orange in the area of a child's bed can be over-stimulating. On the other hand, when a child has low energy or is lethargic, wearing colors at the red end of the spectrum can have a positive, energizing effect.

For educators and those who design school environments, the effects of the various colors can guide color choices for furniture, carpeting, and walls in different areas of the school to produce the desired effect on children given the type of activity that takes place in each area.

Color has also been used in education with children who have difficulty in reading or math. The children use an individually tested colored overlay on the print they are reading and write new words with a different color for each letter (starting in green and ending in red). They use different-colored pens or pencils when working with math problems. Color used in this way helps the children remember more easily and helps to integrate the right and left functions of the brain. (A good reference for using color in learning is Barbara Meister Vitale's book, *Unicorns Are Real*, listed in the Resources section.) In using color with children, it is important to ask them how the color feels for them and if using the color is helping. Children of all ages generally have an accurate sense about the effects of color on them.

There are many more ways in which to use color to help the Dynamic Trio function in a more integrated and balanced way. A place to start exploring the use of color is to become more aware of the colors that surround us and how various colors affect us.

Nature as a Model of Balance

As adults, we are aware of the balancing effects of nature on our minds, bodies, and hearts if we spend time in nature and tune in to its effects on us. Being outside in a natural setting and breathing in clean air can help release toxins. A walk in the woods, sitting by a stream or ocean, being in a grassy meadow, or taking in the light of the moon can be both energizing and calming at the same time. These states work in harmony to produce a sense of wholeness and balance. The colors of nature and their various hues offer a sense of aliveness and balance in their coexistence. In nature we also see the effects of too much water, too strong a wind, too much sun, too much human intervention, etc. on the ecological balance. Thus the effects of imbalance in nature remind us of the inherent importance of a balanced state for all living things.

Providing experiences for children to connect with nature as a way of achieving more balance and/or correcting imbalances is a must in today's society, which has tended to become alienated from the natural world. Experiencing and becoming keen observers of the patterns, balance, and harmony in nature, as well as what happens when the natural balance is upset, can help both children and adults to live in ways that create and support balance. In Chapter 8, the importance of nature in this respect is underscored by the comments of children themselves.

Options for Emotional and Social Balance

We are aware of the significant role that emotions play in supporting the interaction and balance among all the members of the Dynamic Trio. This balance is a critical factor in the well-being, learning, and behavior of children. It is now thought that the development of emotions begins in the womb, at the point when the child can hear sounds and sense the connection with his or her mother. At birth, the child becomes more conscious of interactions with parents through touch, movement, smiles, voice, and responses to needs. Emotions are further developed through interactions with other adults and children in the environment.

As the area for exploration expands for children, they learn about themselves and how to relate to others. Parents, childcare providers, and educators all play critical roles in how children come to view themselves, others, and the world around them. To support the optimal climate for emotional and social development, adults must provide a variety of opportunities and experiences for children that will help them become aware of who they are, manage their emotions and behavior, become self-motivated, develop empathy for others, and develop relationship skills. These areas form the basis for developing the dimensions of emotional intelligence discussed in Chapter 4, The Energy of Emotions.

Children naturally learn some of these skills as they engage in their daily activities. However, in today's society this can be more difficult, as there is often less time for children to engage in creative activities and less opportunity for spontaneous play and informally organized neighborhood games. Now, children are more likely to spend time on the computer,

Chapter 9

playing video games, and watching TV than previous generations of children. Whereas some knowledge and skills can be gained this way, the effects of less quality alone time and less playtime with peers are beginning to emerge. Educators observe less awareness of self and fewer social skills than children had a decade ago. One of the implications of this trend is that adults need to take responsibility for providing more planned experiences that help children attain these emotional intelligence skills at the appropriate times in their development. Following are examples of specific ways that adults can promote the development of emotional and social skills in children:

- Help children become more aware of their feelings by teaching them "feeling" words to connect their thoughts with how their body is responding and their behaviors. This also can be done through the use of pictures, actions, and events that simulate the common experiences they encounter every day. Feeling words that young children can relate to include *happy, sad, angry (mad), scared, excited, loved,* and *worried.* As children become more accustomed to using words to label their feelings, more words can be added.

- Teach children to begin to identify the cause and effect of their emotions as soon as they can understand the concept of cause and effect.

- Help children identify what their individual strengths and talents are and what their limitations are and how to work with them.

- Research anger management, if necessary, to find more ways to help children control their anger, but especially be aware of any underlying causes of ongoing anger problems so they can be addressed.

    Teach children strategies for handling emotionally charged responses of anger and excessive aggression in appropriate ways, such as stopping action and counting to 10, using the HeartMath tool of Freeze Frame, or stopping and taking deep breaths. The following breathing exercise will help children calm negative emotions and reduce stress. They can use it whenever they feel it's necessary throughout the day: Breathe in deeply through the nose, allowing the abdomen to expand, for a count of six to eight. Pause for two counts, then slowly

115

exhale for a count of six to eight, allowing the abdomen to go in again.

Be aware that deep-seated anger may show up as depression or overly controlled emotions, which may at some time erupt.

- Teach children relaxation techniques and peace skills they can use when needed, as well as problem-solving and decision-making skills. (Many good resources are available in these areas, such as *The Whole Kid Peace Activity Book* and *Creating Balance in Children: Activities to Optimize Learning and Behavior,* listed in the Resources section.)

- Create role-play for being with others in different scenarios that are age appropriate by setting up "what to do if ..." situations to help children learn that they have choices about how to respond in social situations. It is important to practice appropriate behaviors in simulated situations so they can be more easily applied when actual situations are encountered.

- Listen to children's dreams. Dreams are one way in which children act out their feelings. Sharing dreams is a way children can get in touch with their feelings to better understand what is currently happening in their lives.

- Help children recognize and respond to the feelings of others by continually modeling these behaviors whenever you can. To assure that this takes place on a consistent basis, adults should have both planned times and spontaneous times when these behaviors are modeled.

- Guide children in reflecting on the effect of their behaviors on others.

- Provide a variety of cooperative learning experiences for children so they can develop social skills in context.

- Help children learn to interpret the facial expressions and body language of others.

- Give as much positive feedback to children as is warranted. When constructive criticism is needed, give it privately, with a

Chapter 9

clear message that it is the behavior that is unacceptable, not the child.

Other ways that adults can be proactive in supporting emotional development and reducing stress in children, especially with regard to learning, are as follows:

- Structure learning experiences that are challenging but are not perceived by children as threatening.

- Pace learning activities (regardless of age) to coincide with the body and mind's ability to sustain focus and need for reflection times to assimilate the learning. A general guideline for optimal focusing time is one minute per year of child's age.

- Provide a balance in activities by varying the amount of structure and choice, allowing for ample movement interspersed with activities such as talking and listening, and reading and creative endeavors.

- Use a variety of techniques, such as stories and role-playing, to help put learning about emotions and social interactions into a meaningful context.

- Learn about and teach children tools such as those provided by the Institute of HeartMath that help reduce stress by bringing the head, heart, and body into a state of balance. (See references in the Resources section.)

- Choose to participate in Families and Schools Together (FAST), a nationally and internationally based program (in 45 states and five countries) for children ages 4-12 and their parents. You may participate as a parent, or you may wish to become a trainer to work in a team to bring the program to families. This program is sponsored by the United States Department of Health and Human Services, Department of Education, and Department of Justice. Improved social skills, better academic performance, and reduced family conflict have been among the significant results for children and parents participating in this program.

The most effective and powerful approach adults can take in helping children achieve more emotional and social balance is to become

Creating Balance in Children's Lives

balanced individuals themselves. By doing this, adults can demonstrate to children approaching tasks and relationships from a balanced state. Young children will initially imitate these behaviors and later understand how to generalize these behaviors to their own situations and lives.

Options for Bringing Out the Spirit in Children

In order to develop balance in children's lives, teachers, parents, and caregivers must bring out the spirit within each child. In the context of this book, spiritual development involves a wide range of inner qualities that can include:

- caring
- curiosity
- passion
- self-worth
- compassion
- courage
- interest
- creativity
- imagination
- intuition
- idealism
- joy
- hope
- love
- wonder
- inspiration
- humor
- enthusiasm
- respect
- reverence
- altruism

Developing these inner qualities of spirit can help foster purpose and the sense of belonging that are so vital to a child's success and happiness. It can help bring meaning to a child's life and put learning into a wider context beyond facts and figures and tests.

In her book *The Soul of Education: Helping Students Find Connection, Compassion, and Character at School,* Rachael Kessler writes: "Students who feel deeply connected don't need danger to feel fully alive. They don't need guns to feel powerful. They don't want to hurt others or themselves. Out of connection grows compassion and passion—passion for people, for students' goals and dreams, for life itself."

Options for developing these qualities are endless, but first and foremost, adults must model them. Then, attention can be given to encouraging these qualities within the context of daily activities and lessons. For example, science lessons can spark awe, reverence, and respect for the marvels of nature, our planet, and the universe. Literature can present models of courage, transformation, and possibility. The arts can enhance creativity and imagination. History can be taught as a fascinating drama of characters and events that provide examples of inner qualities and inspire their cultivation. Math (in fact, all subjects) can be presented in imaginative, fun, and relevant contexts to encourage the development of the child's spirit.

Books and conferences that focus on education and spirituality are listed in the Resource section, so plenty of inspiration is at hand. In providing for this important quadrant in the Wheel of Balance, keep in mind these words of the Dalai Lama: "What is the purpose of life? I believe it is happiness. Our culture, education, economy and all human activities should be meant for that goal."

Other Options for Rebalancing the Dynamic Trio

Numerous other options are available to help bring greater balance into the lives of both adults and children. Discussing all of these options is beyond the scope of this book, but a list of further possibilities is offered below. These are options that generally would fall to the responsibility of parents to pursue. However, educators can benefit from knowing about them so they can collaborate with parents more effectively. It is good to know that many more options for children exist than the use of Ritalin and other drugs, which often have harmful side effects.

Other natural options for adults to explore relative to achieving balance in children include:

- aromatherapy and the use of essential oils
- relaxation techniques and the use of meditation

Creating Balance in Children's Lives

- chiropractic treatment for alignment problems that effect learning and behavior

- other alternative health options, such as acupuncture, acupressure, and homeopathy

- neurofeedback to retrain brainwave states for attention problems and as a relaxation technique

- computer-based options, such as:

    Fast ForWord®, a computer-based training program offered by Scientific Learning Corporation (Oakland, CA), designed to help children become more fluent at processing rapidly changing sounds. These sounds are the building blocks for language and reading development.

    Freeze-Framer®, an interactive, software-based learning program developed by the Institute of HeartMath designed to teach adults and children eight and above to achieve physiological balance, mental clarity, and emotional stability. The program can be used to help people diagnosed with AD/HD improve attention, discrimination, and focus. It also can help adults and children alleviate stress and anxieties, such as students' test, math, and reading anxieties.

    TestEdge™ classroom program and interactive CD-ROM by HeartMath for children in grades 3-6 and 7-12. TestEdge helps children overcome test anxiety and increase their skills in test-taking. They also gain problem-solving, focusing, and listening skills.

Ways to learn more about these options are through the Internet, through books on these topics, and from practitioners who use these techniques with children. As a general guideline, consider using a technique for a child only if it has been proven effective for children of a similar age.

Options Presented in Other Chapters

Many options for helping children achieve balance in learning and behavior have been presented or implied throughout this book. For instance, **Chapter 1** stated that, in general, children's learning styles

Chapter 9

have shifted from mostly auditory and visual to mostly visual and kinesthetic. This is an important reason to increase hands-on learning experiences for children.

Chapter 2 presented a list of ways to make learning more effective, given discoveries about the brain, body, and emotions. This list can be revisited so strategies for education can be based upon these findings.

Chapter 3 confirmed that, generally speaking, whole-brain learning is most effective, using experiences of music, movement, color, visual aids, and auditory input. However, it reminded us that the best way to teach very young children is through imitation, image, emotion, and movement, which are all right-brain functions. The new brain-scan technologies were discussed as useful ways to identify physiological problems and help determine strategies.

Chapter 4 reminded us of the need for creating a supportive emotional climate for effective learning and balanced behavior. This emotional component is so important for children that it should not be considered an option but a requirement. Chapter 4 set the groundwork for the options presented here in Chapter 9.

In **Chapter 5**, Nourishing the Dynamic Trio, many basic needs of children were presented, along with ways to satisfy those needs for healthy functioning and balance in learning and behavior. Refer to this chapter again for many options.

Chapter 6 presented the Wheel of Balance conceptual model that showed the necessity of addressing all the major aspects of a child's life for smooth and balanced functioning. It also provided insights on helping children to achieve "the middle way."

Refer back to **Chapter 7** for a process to help you determine the sources and symptoms of imbalance and thus target options for balance.

In **Chapter 8**, children themselves directly or indirectly suggested options for peace, or balance, such as time with family and friends as well as alone time. Also important to children are nature, animals, books, and music. Further strategies would be to help them solve problems, share their feelings, care about others, and love themselves.

121

Some Final Thoughts

Creating more balance in our lives and in our children's lives is important to our survival and the expansion of human consciousness in the 21st century. As the future of all children lies in what we do to help them in the present, the time to begin this process is now. We need not look far to observe that health, learning, and behavioral imbalances among children are slowing their development and keeping them from reaching their potential. Changes to support and bring more balance into children's lives need to be made at all levels of involvement with children and in all environments in which children participate. In considering the changes that need to be made, let us no longer ask the question, What is wrong with the child? Instead, let us ask the larger question: What is taking place between the people involved, the environment, and the child, and what is happening within the child that is contributing to or causing the observed imbalance?

The information presented in this book is meant to be a catalyst to increase awareness and provide options to consider in evaluating and changing our current parenting and educational practices where change is warranted. This will require an honest approach to being and working with children, a belief in the potential of all children, and an approach that leads from the heart's energy of love. The "quick fix" approach has not worked for the benefit of children. Fortunately, the options available to us now are many and varied. This book is but a beginning. Enjoy the journey of exploring the ideas presented here. Keep an open mind and trust your intuition with regard to what is needed and what to do for yourself and for the children with whom you live and work.

"A child is a person who is going to carry on what you have started. The fate of humanity is in his hands."

Abraham Lincoln

Key Points of Chapter 9

- In a fast-paced lifestyle, it is necessary to allow children sufficient downtime and time for imaginative, creative activities and spontaneous play.

- Studies have confirmed a relationship between what children eat and how they think, act, and learn. It is crucial for parents to look at what they are feeding their families and for schools to evaluate the nutrition of school lunches in order to provide children with balanced meals of quality food. Nutritional strategies, as opposed to drugs, are becoming more widely accepted as treatment options for problems with learning and behavior.

- Movement helps children's sensory-motor development and helps to circulate oxygen and nutrients to all parts of the Dynamic Trio. It helps balance the right and left hemispheres of the brain for greater learning and bring a greater sense of overall balance to the body. It has been reliably demonstrated that movement is critical to a child's state of balance, health, learning, and behavior. Structured movement programs such as Brain Gym, yoga, and tai chi have demonstrated significant improvements in concentration, memory, reading, organization skills, language and number skills, writing, speaking, athletic performance, and overall health.

- Music can inspire, calm, and energize our minds and bodies. It also activates many different parts of the brain, which helps more of the brain's functions to be involved in creating and thinking and facilitates greater balance between the left and right hemispheres of the brain. However, to achieve the benefits of enhanced learning, memory, and energy, it is necessary to choose an appropriate type and volume of music. Music therapy has been found to be effective in reducing stress and facilitating the healing of mental conditions and various illnesses of the body.

- When we are deprived of natural light and/or the frequencies of the full spectrum of colors, our health, moods, and mental capacities are negatively affected. Children's behavior, class performance, and overall achievement have been shown to improve significantly in classrooms with full-spectrum lighting. Scientists and practitioners use color to facilitate learning and change behavior, and they also use color for healing purposes. Parents can help children choose appropriate colors to wear and select appropriate colors for areas where children play and sleep. Educators and designers of school environments should consider the effects of various colors in designing and decorating different activity areas.

Creating Balance in Children's Lives

- Nature has balancing effects on our minds, bodies, and hearts. Providing experiences for children to connect with nature as a way of achieving more balance and/or correcting imbalances is a must in today's society, which has tended to become alienated from the natural world.

- Adults need to provide more opportunities and experiences that help children attain emotional intelligence skills, such as becoming aware of who they are, managing their emotions and behavior, becoming self-motivated, developing empathy for others, and developing relationship skills.

- The most effective and powerful approach adults can take in helping children achieve more emotional and social balance is to become balanced individuals themselves.

- Alternative health options, neurofeedback, and computer-based options for balancing are increasingly available.

- We need to ask not what is wrong with the child, but to ask what is taking place between the people, the environment, and the child, and what is happening within the child that is contributing to or causing the observed imbalance.

- Creating more balance in our own lives and in our children's lives is vital to our survival and the expansion of human consciousness in the 21st century.

OPTIONS AT A GLANCE

Following is an overview of the options for creating balance in children's lives that are covered more fully in the main text of this book.

- Help the child achieve balance between the physical, mental, emotional, and spiritual aspects of life.

- Provide a good role model of balance.

- When an imbalance is evident in a child's learning or behavior, use a logical process to sort through and identify potential sources of stress, test your hypotheses, and determine ways to alleviate the problem/s. (See process in Chapter 7.)

- Engage both hemispheres of the brain in the learning process (logical, analytical, linear + creative, intuitive, spatial).

- Provide the child with plenty of mental stimulation.

- When possible, present information within a context rather than as discrete facts.

- Consider the child's preferred learning style (visual, auditory, kinesthetic).

- When possible, present learning through multisensory experiences.

- For very young children, emphasize right-brain learning through imitation, image, emotion, and movement.

- Actively engage the learner.

- If possible, make educational material relevant to a child's life.

- Provide immediate feedback where possible.

- Provide a challenging, but safe and nonthreatening, environment that incorporates positive emotional support and a sense of fun and exploration.

Creating Balance in Children's Lives

- Provide input at a level of difficulty that is appropriate for the child at his or her stage of development.

- In providing for a child's needs, consider not only the normative growth patterns of children but the unique qualities and needs of the particular child.

- Give the child choices and a degree of control.

- Encourage the child to develop a broad range of skills and interests that are mental, physical, emotional, aesthetic, and social.

- Allow the child sufficient time for imaginative and creative activities and spontaneous play.

- Be aware of a child's emotional state, and help reduce or eliminate conditions that may be causing mental, emotional, or physical stress in the child's life.

- Provide plenty of positive emotional support in terms of love and encouragement.

- By modeling and providing opportunities to do so, help the child develop emotional intelligence: self-awareness, self-control, self-motivation, empathy, and relationship skills.

- Support the child's brain and the rest of the body with a diet that supplies adequate protein, carbohydrates, "good" fats, vitamins, minerals, and calories.

- Make sure the child eats a good breakfast.

- Limit fast foods, processed foods, sugar, caffeinated soft drinks, and aspartame.

- Consider nutritional strategies, as opposed to drugs, as treatment options for problems with learning and behavior.

- As much as possible, make sure the child receives plenty of clean air, pure water, and natural light. Consider using full-spectrum lighting indoors.

Options at a Glance

- Make sure the child gets enough sleep, rest, and restful activity as well as enough exercise.

- Consider structured movement programs to alleviate learning and behavior problems.

- Provide a wide variety of sensory stimulation, but avoid extremes (such as loud sounds) on a regular basis.

- Limit TV watching and video games.

- Help the child achieve the "middle way" and a flow of energy between opposites and extremes.

- Help the child achieve a balance between alone time and time with others, and a balance between different types of activities.

- Help the child solve problems, share his or her feelings, care about others, and love him- or herself.

- Make sure the child has access to nature and animals.

- Provide the child with good books and music.

- Consider the use of aromatherapy for the treatment of depression, agitation, anxiety, and hyperactivity.

- Consider music therapy for reducing stress and facilitating the healing of various illnesses of the body and mental conditions.

- Use color to facilitate learning or healing, change behavior, and enhance certain mental states, moods, and activities.

- When appropriate, consider alternative health options, such as chiropractic, homeopathy, acupuncture, and acupressure.

- Consider neurofeedback for retraining brainwave states to enhance attention and relaxation.

- When appropriate, consider computer-based options, such as Fast ForWord, Freeze-Framer, and TestEdge.

Notes

GLOSSARY

The following are functional definitions related to the context of this book.

amygdala—a structure in the brain that filters and interprets incoming sensory information in the context of our survival and emotional needs and helps initiate appropriate responses. The amygdala is part of the limbic system in the mammalian brain, or mid-brain, which deals with emotions.

aromatherapy—the use of aromas in essential oils extracted from herbs, flowers, and fruits to enhance a person's well-being

autism—a developmental disorder characterized by an impairment in reciprocal social interactions and in verbal and/or nonverbal communication

autonomic nervous system—the part of the nervous system that controls all involuntary functions within the body. This system includes two branches: the sympathetic and parasympathetic.

axon—the extension from the main cell body of a neuron that sends information to other cells

brainwave state—a pattern of electrical current in the brain that determines a person's state of awareness, ranging from an alert, waking state (beta) to deep sleep (delta). Brainwave states are also called states of consciousness.

central nervous system—the part of the nervous system that includes the brain and spinal cord. The central nervous system coordinates the activity of the entire nervous system.

decibel (dBA)—one degree of loudness on a continuum of sound where zero represents the least perceptible sound and about 130 decibels is the pain level of sound

dendrite—one of the spidery branches extending from the main cell body of a neuron that receives information from other cells

dyslexia—a learning disorder that involves difficulty processing language and is usually manifested through problems with reading, writing, and spelling

dyspraxia—a condition characterized by difficulty with motor coordination

frontal lobes—the pair of lobes in the neocortex of the brain that are involved with judgment, creativity, decision-making, and planning

functional magnetic resonance imaging (fMRI)—a noninvasive diagnostic technique using radio waves that produces computerized images of internal body tissues. An MRI of the brain can reveal where functional problems lie.

hippocampus—a structure in the brain that relates what is happening in the present to memories of past experiences and converts important short-term memory into long-term memory. The hippocampus is part of the limbic system, which deals with emotions.

hypothalamus—a structure in the brain that monitors internal regulatory systems, informs the brain of activities within the body, and links the prefrontal cortex of the brain with the nervous and endocrine systems. The hypothalamus is part of the limbic system.

left hemisphere—the left side of the brain, which is the seat of language, logic, interpretation, and sequential processing

limbic system—parts of the brain including the thalamus, hypothalamus, hippocampus, and amygdala that are concerned especially with emotions and motivation. The limbic system is often called the mammalian brain or the mid-brain.

neocortex—the thinking part of the brain, which includes four pairs of lobes: frontal, parietal, temporal, and occipital lobes

neural pathway—part of the network of nerve cells along which neurotransmitters carry information and messages

neuroscience—the branch of the life sciences that deals with the central nervous system, especially as it relates to learning and behavior

neurofeedback—a computerized method of assessing and consciously changing brainwave states, or patterns

Glossary

neuron—the main kind of cell that makes up the tissue in the brain and central nervous system. A neuron sends and receives information by means of electrical and chemical signals.

neuroglia (glia, or glial cells)—cells that provide supporting tissue for neurons in the central nervous system

neurotransmitter—one of the brain's chemical messengers

nervous system—the system in a vertebrate's body that includes the brain, spinal cord, nerves, ganglia, and parts of receptor organs. The nervous system receives and interprets stimuli and transmits impulses throughout the body. It is made up of the central nervous system and the peripheral nervous system.

occipital lobes—the pair of lobes in the neocortex of the brain that are involved with processing visual stimuli

parasympathetic nervous system—the branch of the autonomic nervous system involved with relaxation

parietal lobes—the pair of lobes in the neocortex of the brain that are involved with sensations of touch, temperature, pain, and pressure, and also with spatial awareness of body parts in relation to the surroundings

peptides—neurotransmitters of a certain kind that play important roles in modulating emotional states and consequent behaviors. Peptides are located throughout the body.

peripheral nervous system—the part of the nervous system that is outside the central nervous system and includes the autonomic nervous system

positron-emission tomography (PET)—a method of obtaining cross-sectional images of a specific area of body metabolism by injecting a metabolic substance that includes positively charged particles

right hemisphere—the right side of the brain, which is the seat of nonverbal processes, visual pattern recognition (faces, lines, shapes), and spatial skills

Creating Balance in Children's Lives

stress—the physiological and psychological effects on the body and mind in response to intense external stimuli

survival brain—the part of the brain involved with those functions necessary for survival, including the fight-or-flight response. The survival brain is also called the reptilian or old brain. It includes the brain stem and the cerebellum.

sympathetic nervous system—the branch of the autonomic nervous system involved with arousal, excitation, and action

synapse—the junction point where a nerve impulse is transferred between cells

temporal lobes—the pair of lobes in the neocortex of the brain that are involved with interpretation of auditory stimuli

thalamus—a structure in the limbic system of the brain that is a major relay station for incoming stimuli and informs the brain of external stimuli. The thalamus directs sensory information to the lobes of the neocortex and any emotionally laden information to the amygdala for response.

yin/yang—complementary energies that represent the relationship of opposites, such as completion (yin) and creation (yang), and contraction (yin) and expansion (yang)

RESOURCES

Books

Aggleton, John P., ed. *The Amygdala: Neurobiological Aspects of Emotion, Memory, and Mental Dysfunction.* New York: Wiley-Liss, 1992.

Amen, Daniel, G., M.D. *Change Your Brain Change Your Life: The Breakthrough Program for Conquering Anxiety, Depression, Obsessiveness, Anger, and Impulsiveness.* New York: Times Books, 1998.

Amen, Daniel, G., M.D. *Healing ADD: The Breakthrough Program That Allows You to See and Heal the Six Types of Attention Deficit Disorder.* New York: G. P. Putnam's Sons, 2001.

Ayres, A. Jean, Ph.D. *Sensory Integration and the Child.* Los Angeles: Western Psychological Services, 1987.

Bove, Mary, N.D. *An Encyclopedia of Natural Healing for Children and Infants.* Chicago: Keats Pub., 2001.

Campbell, Don G. *The Mozart Effect: Tapping the Power of Music to Heal the Body, Strengthen the Mind, and Unlock the Creative Spirit.* New York: Avon Books, 1997.

Campbell, Don G. *The Mozart Effect for Children: Awakening Your Child's Mind, Health, and Creativity with Music.* New York: HarperCollins Publishers, Inc., 2000.

Carroll, Lee, and Jan Tober. *The Indigo Children: The New Kids Have Arrived.* Carlsbad, California: Hay House, Inc., 1999.

Childre, Doc Lew. *Teaching Children to Love: 80 Games & Fun Activities for Raising Balanced Children in Unbalanced Times.* Boulder Creek, California: Planetary Publications, 1996.

Childre, Doc, and Howard Martin, with Donna Beech. *The HeartMath Solution: The Institute of HeartMath's Revolutionary Program for Engaging the Power of the Heart's Intelligence.* New York: HarperCollins Publishers, Inc., 1999.

Coles, Robert. *The Spiritual Life of Children.* Boston: Houghton Mifflin Company, 1990.

Dennison, Paul E., Ph.D., and Gail E. Hargrave. *Personalized Whole Brain Integration: The Basic II Manual on Educational Kinesiology.* Glendale, California: Edu-Kinesthetics, Inc., 1985.

Diamond, Marian, Ph.D., and Janet Hopson. *Magic Trees of the Mind: How to Nurture Your Child's Intelligence, Creativity, and Healthy Emotions from Birth Through Adolescence.* New York: Penguin Putman, Inc., 1998.

Dryden, Gordon, and Jeannette Vos, Ph.D. *The Learning Revolution: To Change the Way the World Learns.* Torrance, California: The Learning Web, 1999. (New, updated version due 2004)

Eliot, Lise, Ph.D. *What's Going On in There?: How the Brain and Mind Develop in the First Five Years of Life.* New York: Bantam Books, 1999.

Elkind, David, Ph.D. *The Hurried Child: Growing Up Too Fast Too Soon.* Cambridge, Massachusetts: Perseus Publishing, 2001.

Gardner, Howard. *Frames of Mind: The Theory of Multiple Intelligences.* New York: Basic Books, Inc., 1983.

Gardner, Howard. *Intelligence Reframed: Multiple Intelligences for the 21st Century.* New York: Basic Books, 2000.

Glazer, Steven. *The Heart of Learning: Spirituality in Education.* New York: Putnam Publishing Group, 1999.

Goleman, Daniel. *Emotional Intelligence: Why It Can Matter More than IQ.* New York: Bantam Books, 1995.

Hannaford, Carla, Ph.D. *Awakening the Child Heart: Handbook for Global Parenting.* Captain Cook, Hawaii: Jamilla Nur Publishing, 2002.

Hannaford, Carla, Ph.D. *Smart Moves: Why Learning Is Not All in Your Head.* Atlanta, Georgia: Great Ocean Publishers, 1995.

Healy, Jane M., Ph.D. *Endangered Minds: Why Children Don't Think— and What We Can Do About It.* New York: Touchstone Books, 1999.

Heller, Sharon, Ph.D. *Too Loud, Too Bright, Too Fast, Too Tight: What to Do If You Are Sensory Defensive in an Overstimulating World.* New York: HarperCollins Publishers, Inc., 2002.

Henrikson, Peggy, and Lorraine O. Moore, Ph.D., with Linda LeClaire and Pamela S. Welter. *The Whole Kid Peace Activity Book: Promoting Self-Esteem, Preventing Conflict.* Eden Prairie, Minnesota: PeaceStar Publishing, 1997. Distributed by Peytral Publications, Inc., Minnetonka, Minnesota.

Houston, Jean, Ph.D. *Jump Time: Shaping Your Future in a World of Radical Change.* New York: Penguin Putnam Inc., 2000.

Hubert, Bill. *Bal-A-Vis-X: Rhythmic Balance/Auditory/Vision eXercises for Brain and Brain-Body Integration.* Wichita, Kansas: Bal-A-Vis-X, Inc., 2001.

Jensen, Eric. *Teaching with the Brain in Mind.* Alexandria, Virginia: Association for Supervision and Curriculum Development, 1998.

Kessler, Rachael. *The Soul of Education: Helping Students Find Connection, Compassion, and Character at School.* Alexandria, Virginia: Association for Supervision and Curriculum Development, 2000.

Kotulak, Ronald. *Inside the Brain: Revolutionary Discoveries of How the Mind Works.* Kansas City, Missouri: Andrews McMeel Publishing, 1997.

Lantieri, Linda. *Schools with Spirit: Nurturing the Lives of Children and Teachers.* Boston: Beacon Press, 2002.

Levine, Mel, M.D. *A Mind at a Time: America's Top Learning Expert Shows How Every Child Can Succeed.* New York: Simon & Schuster, 2002.

Mallon, Brenda. *Dream Time with Children: Learning to Dream, Dreaming to Learn.* Philadelphia: Jessica Kingsley Publishers, 2002.

Moore, Lorraine O., Ph.D., and Peggy Henrikson. *Creating Balance in Children: Activities to Optimize Learning and Behavior.* Minnetonka, Minnesota: Peytral Publications, Inc., 2005.

Moore, Lorraine O., Ph.D. *Inclusion: A Practical Guide for Parents—Tools to Enhance Your Child's Success in Learning.* Minnetonka, Minnesota: Peytral Publications, Inc., 2000.

Moore, Lorraine O., Ph.D. *Inclusion: Strategies for Working with Young Children—A Resource Guide for Teachers, Childcare Providers, and Parents.* Minnetonka, Minnesota: Peytral Publications, Inc., 2003.

Olson, Stuart Alve. *Tai Chi for Kids: Move with the Animals.* Rochester, Vermont: Bear Cub Books, 2001.

Ostrander, Sheila, and Lynn Schroeder, with Nancy Ostrander. *Superlearning 2000: New Triple-Fast Ways You Can Learn, Earn, and Succeed in the 21st Century.* New York: Delacorte Press, 1994.

Palmer, Parket J. *To Know as We Are Known: Education as a Spiritual Journey.* San Francisco: HarperSanFrancisco, 1993.

Pearce, Joseph Chilton. *Evolution's End: Claiming the Potential of Our Intelligence.* San Francisco: HarperSanFrancisco, 1993.

Pert, Candace B., Ph.D. *Molecules of Emotion: The Science Behind Mind-Body Medicine.* New York: Simon and Schuster, 1999.

Ratey, John J., M.D. *A User's Guide to the Brain: Perception, Attention, and the Four Theaters of the Brain.* New York: Vintage Books, 2002.

Restak, Richard, M.D. *The Secret Life of the Brain.* Washington, D.C.: Joseph Henry Press, 2001.

Roberts, H. J., M.D. *Aspartame Disease, an Ignored Epidemic.* West Palm Beach, Florida: Sunshine Sentinel Press, Inc., 2001.

Satter, Ellyn. *How to Get Your Kid to Eat . . . But Not Too Much (from Birth to Adolescence).* Boulder, Colorado: Bull Publishing Company, 1987.

Satter, Ellyn. *Secrets of Feeding a Healthy Family.* Madison, Wisconsin: Kelcy Press, 1999.

Resources

Sears, William, M.D., and Martha Sears, R.N. *The Family Nutrition Book: Everything You Need to Know About Feeding Your Children—from Birth Through Adolescence.* Boston: Little, Brown and Company, 1999.

Sears, William, M.D., and Peter Sears, M.D., with Sean Foy, M.A. *Dr. Sears' Lean Kids: A Total Health Program for Children Ages 6-12.* New York: New American Library, 2003.

Sousa, David A. *How the Brain Learns: A Classroom Teacher's Guide.* Thousand Oaks, California: Corwin Press, Inc., 2001.

Sousa, David A. *How the Special Needs Brain Learns.* Thousand Oaks, California: Corwin Press, Inc., 2001.

Stordy, B. Jacqueline, Ph.D., and Malcolm J. Nicholl, Ph.D. *The LCP Solution: The Remarkable Nutritional Treatment for ADHD, Dyslexia & Dyspraxia.* New York: Ballantine Books, 2000.

Sumar, Sonia. *Yoga for the Special Child: A Therapeutic Approach for Infants and Children with Down Syndrome, Cerebral Palsy, and Learning Disabilities.* Buckingham, Virginia: Special Yoga Publications, 1998.

Sylwester, Robert. *A Celebration of Neurons: An Educator's Guide to the Human Brain.* Alexandria, Virginia: Association for Supervision and Curriculum Development, 1995.

Tobias, Cynthia Ulrich. *The Way They Learn: How to Discover and Teach to Your Child's Strengths.* Colorado Springs, Colorado: Focus on the Family Pub., 1998.

Vitale, Barbara Meister. *Unicorns Are Real: A Right-Brained Approach to Learning.* Rolling Hills Estates, California: Jalmar Press, 1982. (Can be ordered through *http://www.barbaravitale.com*.)

Willett, Walter C., and The Harvard School of Public Health. *Eat, Drink, and Be Healthy: The Harvard Medical School Guide to Healthy Eating.* New York: Free Press, 2003.

Wise, Anna. *The High-Performance Mind: Mastering Brainwaves for Insight, Healing, and Creativity.* New York: Jeremy P. Tarcher/Putnam, 1995.

Creating Balance in Children's Lives

Witkin, Georgia, Ph.D. *KidStress: What It Is, How It Feels, How to Help.* New York: Penguin USA, 2000.

Wolfe, Patricia. *Brain Matters: Translating Research into Classroom Practice.* Alexandria, Virginia: Association for Supervision and Curriculum Development, 2001.

Web Sites

Brain Gym®:
http://www.braingym.org

Families and Schools Together (FAST):
http://www.wcer.wisc.edu/fast

Gesell Institute of Human Development:
http://www.gesellinstitute.org

Institute of HeartMath:
http://www.heartmath.org

National Institutes of Health:
http://www.nih.gov

Neuroscience for Kids:
http://faculty.washington.edu/chudler/neurok.html

U.S. Environmental Protection Agency:
http://www.epa.gov
http://www.epa.gov/kids
http://www.epa.gov/schools
http://www.epa.gov/iaq/schools ("Indoor Air Quality: Tools for Schools")
http://www.epa.gov/iaq/homes

World Natural Health Organization:
http://www.wnho.net

Resources

Conferences on Spirituality, Education, and Children

ChildSpirit: Exploring and Nurturing the Spiritual World of Children and Youth
Annual North American Conference on Children's Spirituality
www.childspirit.net

Annual International Conference on Education, Spirituality and the Whole Child
Roehampton University, London
www.roehampton.ac.uk

Holistic Education Network: Conferences and Discussion of Related Interest
Tasmania, Australia
Conferences around the world that relate to holistic education
www.hent.org

Notes

Notes

Notes

Notes

Notes

Notes

Notes

Notes

Notes

Notes

Notes